Leading Peak Performance: Lessons from the Wild Dogs of Africa

How to Create Pack Leadership and
Produce Transformative Results

Also available from ASQ Quality Press:

Transformational Leadership: Creating Organizations of Meaning
Stephen Hacker and Tammy Roberts

The Trust Imperative: Performance Improvement Through Productive Relationships
Marsha Willard and Stephen Hacker

The Certified Manager of Quality/Organizational Excellence Handbook: Third Edition
Russell T. Westcott, editor

Avoiding the Corporate Death Spiral: Recognizing and Eliminating the Signs of Decline
Gregg Stocker

The Magic of Self-Directed Work Teams: A Case Study in Courage and Culture Change
Paul C. Palmes

Everyday Excellence: Creating a Better Workplace through Attitude, Action, and Appreciation
Clive Shearer

Making Change Work: Practical Tools for Overcoming Human Resistance to Change
Brien Palmer

Business Performance through Lean Six Sigma: Linking the Knowledge Worker, the Twelve Pillars, and Baldrige
James T. Schutta

Leadership For Results: Removing Barriers to Success for People, Projects, and Processes
Tom Barker

Managing with Conscience for Competitive Advantage
Pete Geissler

Quality Makes Money: How to Involve Every Person on the Payroll in a Complete Quality Process (CQP)
Pat Townsend and Joan Gebhardt

Quality management — Guidelines for realizing financial and economic benefits
ANSI/ISO/ASQ Q10014-2006

To request a complimentary catalog of ASQ Quality Press publications, call 800-248-1946, or visit our Web site at http://qualitypress.asq.org.

Leading Peak Performance: Lessons from the Wild Dogs of Africa

How to Create Pack Leadership and Produce Transformative Results

Stephen Hacker and
Marvin Washington

ASQ Quality Press
Milwaukee, Wisconsin

American Society for Quality, Quality Press, Milwaukee, WI 53203
© 2007 by ASQ
All rights reserved. Published 2007.
Printed in the United States of America.

13 12 11 10 09 08 07   5 4 3 2 1

Library of Congress Cataloging-in-Publication Data

Hacker, Stephen, 1955-
  Leading peak performance : lessons from the wild dogs of Africa / Stephen
Hacker and Marvin Washington.
    p. cm.
Includes bibliographical references and index.
ISBN 978-0-87389-708-2 -- ISBN 978-0-87389-701-3
1. Teams in the workplace--Management. 2. Self-directed work teams
3. Performance--Psychological aspects. 4. Leadership--Evaluation.
5. Organizational effectiveness I. Washington, Marvin. II. Title. III.
Title: Pack leadership.

  HD66.H327 2007
  658.4'022--dc22
                                2007002459
  ISBN-13: 978-0-87389-708-2

Publisher: William A. Tony
Acquisitions Editor: Matt T. Meinholz
Project Editor: Paul O'Mara
Production Administrator: Randall Benson

ASQ Mission: The American Society for Quality advances individual,
organizational, and community excellence worldwide through learning,
quality improvement, and knowledge exchange.

Attention Bookstores, Wholesalers, Schools, and Corporations: ASQ Quality
Press books, videotapes, audiotapes, and software are available at quantity
discounts with bulk purchases for business, educational, or instructional use.
For information, please contact ASQ Quality Press at 800-248-1946, or write
to ASQ Quality Press, P.O. Box 3005, Milwaukee, WI 53201-3005.

To place orders or to request a free copy of the ASQ Quality Press Publications
Catalog, including ASQ membership information, call 800-248-1946. Visit our
Web site at www.asq.org or http://qualitypress.asq.org.

∞ Printed on acid-free paper

Quality Press
600 N. Plankinton Avenue
Milwaukee, Wisconsin 53203
Call toll free 800-248-1946
Fax 414-272-1734
www.asq.org
http://www.asq.org/quality-press
http://standardsgroup.asq.org
E-mail: authors@asq.org

ASQ
AMERICAN SOCIETY
FOR QUALITY

Contents

Foreword

During my time as CEO of COLA, an international healthcare organization, I have seen many changes in the U. S. healthcare system and I believe that this is just the beginning. The mission of COLA has long been to improve the quality and safety of laboratory medicine and patient care, but many laboratories have begun using less-skilled personnel to perform simplified methods of testing. They don't see a need for COLA to help them improve quality. With these and other changes in healthcare, it is more and more difficult to have an impact. COLA has been on the decline. In ten years, COLA's marketplace of clinical laboratories decreased by more than 40 percent.

At one point it occurred to me that COLA would have to change, and that my leadership style would have to change as well. Both the organization and its leader would be required to transform in order to survive. With that revelation, we set out to capitalize on our strengths and reinvent ourselves in other areas. We recognized that only by changing our perspective could we redefine the robust value COLA has to offer the world. We adopted a different mindset, broadened our talent base, and became more creative in our efforts to meet our collective vision. We went beyond our comfort zone.

Transforming ourselves and our organizations is never an easy task. It requires new ways of thinking that may be outside of our personal and professional experience. In the past, our mental models helped us to isolate problems, engage others in solving them, and get on with business. It's sometimes difficult to adopt new ways of thinking, but relying solely on what we have always known often produces outcomes that are no longer relevant in the changing world.

As the world evolves, we often find ourselves swimming in unfamiliar waters. Success in a world filled with unknowns most often occurs with the application of new concepts. Success results from examining familiar mental models, rejecting those that no longer serve, and then moving on to new areas of thought. This may feel risky, but it's worth the effort.

Books that reinforce what I already know are of limited value. Books that require me to re-think my assumptions and to adopt new mental models offer the most value. This book challenged my thinking about leadership, community, teams, and organizations, and these leadership concepts offered fresh insight.

I have long understood the advantages and disadvantages of the command-and-control model of leadership, and I studied the concept of empowerment that emerged in the eighties. Both paradigms fall short of what I need in this evolving world, so one of the key ideas I took from this book has to do with pack leadership. I discovered on my own journey that the best way to lead is to have others join me on the hunt. Wild dog leadership is the alternative I had been searching for.

Pack leadership isn't about giving up your power, it's about inviting others to join you as you collectively lead your organization. This may seem obvious, but an intellectual understanding of the concept is not the same as living it. It's the difference between giving lip service to a concept and holding it as a core principle of highest import. To really get there, you must jettison old, unconscious habits.

To further expand our reach at COLA, we needed to form a world community where others sharing our vision could take the lead. We put out the call to diverse, committed leaders, asking them to come together to explore ways to improve laboratory medicine and patient care around the world. We gathered together because we all faced urgent needs, including public health crises, and held as our collective goal the improvement in the quality of patient care.

To create worldwide societal transformation in healthcare, we realized that pack vision would be required, along with a strong spirit of community and powerful individual contributors with the tenacity to follow through on making the vision a reality.

Within the spirit of community and in alignment with the pack vision, partnerships have now formed that go beyond traditional rules of engagement. Rather than being based primarily on transactions of value, these partnerships are sourced in a shared commitment to realizing the pack vision. Efforts are further fueled by the idea of being part of a larger movement to actually transform healthcare. No more tinkering with the edges; we share a commitment to creating a profound shift in the system.

This is COLA's way to expand its mission and its impact on the world. It would not be possible without a community of leaders coming together to act. Our international 'pack of wild dogs'–the World Lab Forum–is on the hunt, determined to make a profound impact on the quality of laboratory medicine worldwide.

It is my pleasure and honor to be considered a part of this movement toward transformational change. I welcome this significant effort to move the body of knowledge forward.

Doug Beigel
CEO, COLA

Preface

Wild dogs? Wild dogs? How can a book about wild dogs help me become a better leader? We know that those may be some of the thoughts going through your head as you look at the title of our book. First, the facts: Guess which predator is the best at killing its target. It's not the lion; it's not the cheetah. Did you guess? It's the wild dog of Africa. Wild dogs make a successful kill 80 percent of the time, whereas the lion and cheetah are successful less than 50 percent of the time. This book translates the success characteristics of the wild dogs of Africa into actions and behaviors that can make you a more productive leader with a more effective leadership team.

If you are still reading, you are now probably thinking, *"Why do I need another book on leadership? Aren't there already enough? Hasn't this subject been exhausted, thoroughly researched, and suitably documented? Why should I read another book?"*

We, the authors, have asked ourselves these same questions upon seeing yet another leadership text while browsing through bookstores. Donald Trump has five books, Charles Schwab has penned five, Andy Grove has four, Bill Gates two, and Jack Welch two. Some of the best-selling titles cover leadership lessons from Moses to the Third Reich, from *The Art of War* to *Jesus as CEO*. It seems as if the topic has been thoroughly discussed. What can another book on leadership offer?

Having read, studied, and researched extensively on the subject, we too look with a cynical eye at the value of reading another 'airport book' about leadership. Offered are a slick cover and some over-the-top testimonials about how others were brought to great wisdom and achievement upon reading the first few pages. But with the nudge of curiosity, the book is opened. Although often approached with a skeptic's eye, the new book may provide some insights and may offer enough appeal to read on. A new concept, a different perspective, or something that triggers further research may come from the read. Despite the hesitation, our understanding of leadership grows. Given that we almost always gain some new insight, why do we hesitate to read another leadership book?

The answer to that question can be found in the changing face of effective leadership. Leadership is a dynamic subject, shifting and adapting to the latest social structures, followers, technologies, and performance requirements of the times. Technology, globalization, hyper-competition, empowerment ideas, and other influences periodically have forced experienced leaders to adopt new leadership skills and paradigms or become outdated.

In part, this forced adaptation by leaders is driven by the people they lead. The evolving characteristics and needs of followers necessitate the continual refinement of leadership. In the free and developed countries of the twenty-first century, followers have access to extensive information. This information compares favorably to the amount and accuracy of the information leadership itself commands. Access to education, funding, power, and influence all are much greater for the followers of today than for the followers of but a decade ago.

The convergence of technological, social, and political change keeps the subject of leadership vibrant. Of even greater impact is the way business, civic, religious, and other leaders are integrating these new tools and ideas in a collective manner. The breakneck speed at which we share concepts, mental models, and approaches, combined with the amount of time we immerse ourselves in study, has produced an emerging understanding of the challenges of leadership. Society as a whole produces an ever-expanding collective consciousness about effective and ineffective leadership. This evolution of collective consciousness brings forth new leadership ideas, models, experimentation, and performance expectations. Society continues to witness shifts in the paradigm of leadership. In this context, a paradigm, or world view, is a set of assumptions that individuals develop in a lifetime[1]. Paradigms aren't inherently good or bad, but they can become ineffective if never modernized. As the world changes, so do our paradigms about how the world operates. Thus, new leadership concepts are needed to address these new paradigms.

Often, the put-off in learning about shifts in leadership thinking and practices is caused by the promise of the last leadership book or program encountered. Leadership books and programs often project themselves as the Holy Grail at the end of a long and exhaustive journey. A definitive leadership philosophy is often put forth. But the insights frequently fall short of expectations and often holes in the theory become apparent when applied to present day situations. Maybe this is where the hesitation comes from for reading 'yet another leadership book.'

Our focus connects leadership to performance. Somewhere in the profusion of leadership texts, the concept of performance was dropped. The search started with the desire to find the best performers and then identify their leadership skills. But now it seems that authors, many of whom are leaders writing about their own journeys, have placed more emphasis on personality and leadership insights than on identifying broad characteristics or skills that can be applied by current or aspiring leaders. What is needed is the identification of leadership characteristics that produce great performance, not just another book on leadership wisdoms written by a great leadership personality. We really care about a study of leadership in as much as the behaviors, characteristics, and skills identified produce higher levels of performance.

We enter into the spirited and feisty discussion of leadership for the sake of advancing the collective knowledge about effective leadership in a constantly changing world. We hope to make a meaningful contribution to the body of knowledge on leadership today and for the near future. As the world moves, so do the requirements of organizational leaders. We make our contribution using as our primary vehicle the wild dogs of Africa and the concept of the pack, a unique team archetype. We developed this analogy over a seven-year period during our trips to game preserves in Botswana and South Africa, where we worked on a large-scale change effort within the public sector of Botswana. The common denominator for animals in the wild is their focus on a single goal: survival. The traits, characteristics, and behaviors of the animals that are most successful in survival led us to think about how these skills could be transferred to human groups. After observing zebras, elephants, lions, and cheetahs, we became increasingly interested in the success of the African wild dog and fashioned our analogy around their performance. As we will show, it is the leadership traits of the wild dog that we believe are most needed for today's leadership challenges. We seek lessons for today's leaders demonstrated by these unique animals and their interactions.

We rely on this analogy throughout our book because analogies offer a means to enhance understanding of ourselves. An *analogy* is an inference that if two or more things agree with one another in some respects, they will probably agree in others. An analogy is also a resemblance in some particulars between things that are otherwise unlike. Analogies facilitate a deeper connection with others who hold shared knowledge of the analogy's relevance, creating power in the language of a group or organization. An analogy allows us to discover similarities when comparing two seemingly unlike things by inferring resemblances in certain areas. Analogies help us cut through the complexities of concept and offer insight to the concept's functional basis. Analogies offer the power of simplification and identification with a readily understood surrogate.

The power of an analogy can also be a ground of weakness. The topics of leadership and people are complex and the wild dogs do not accurately represent the totality of human beings within organizations. We do not recommend that you emulate the wild dogs in total in your efforts to grow in leadership ability: move to Africa, travel naked, eat your food raw, and live in a cave. We advise readers to take away the applicable lessons and leave behind an exhaustive analysis of the comparison. Focus on gaining personal insights to increase your leadership abilities and hold off from making an exact fit with the animal world.

We see this contribution and our lessons from the wild animal kingdom as but pieces of leadership discussions currently underway. More specific leadership learnings can be found in particular applications. Our goal is to show how this analogy seems to make sense of the current reality of leadership including the problems and solutions faced by leaders.

We believe that great leaders have a deep sense of who they are; we call this self mastery. Self mastery encompasses a strong sense of self (understanding how I act and think) and personal performance (understanding my connection to the larger solution). Based upon our own self mastery, we admit, unfortunately, that this may not be the last word on leadership, nor is it likely to be the last book on leadership that you will ever buy. Therefore, the study of leadership fundamentals does not disappear. Our intent is to spur your thinking about new ideas of leadership by presenting our understanding the complexity of today's problems, followers, and solutions.

We trust you will benefit from this reading and quickly assemble a pack of wild dogs within your organization. You may also discover the wild dog persona to have benefits beyond the workplace. If you are the leader of any team, inside or outside of the workplace, this book will provide leadership insights and offer tangible methods for improving your team's effectiveness.

We invite you to discover lessons about leadership in the pages that follow. We structure each chapter in a similar fashion. After discussing each topic, we provide summary points and action opportunities so that you can practice your newly learned concepts. In the first appendix, we present the research, both academic and field-related, that helped to ensure the analogy was more than just a good talk, that it also had some merit. In the second and third appendix, we provide two assessment tools that can help you and your group or team gain deeper insights into your leadership style. We also provide a collection of wild dog case studies at the end of some of the chapters to show how the concepts of pack leadership operate in a variety of organizational and team settings. We think that you will start seeing wild dogs everywhere once you understand the analogy and develop an appreciation for the traits of the wild dog.

NOTE

1. Joel A. Barker; *Discovering the Future: The Business of Paradigms* (Charthouse International Learning Corporation video, 1990).

Acknowledgements

SPECIAL NOTES OF APPRECIATION GO TO:

Tammy Roberts – Her role as 'book boss' was instrumental in bringing this work to publication. Additionally, her editing and guidance concerning content flow were of enormous value. As a friend, colleague, and creative spirit, she is valued beyond these few words of thanks.

The Performance Center (TPC) community – This learning community has contributed greatly to our evolving understanding of transformation in the broadest sense.

The Transformation Systems International (TSI) community – Only through the reaction to practice opportunities provided by this community of practitioners, university faculty, and clients could we have had the courage to stand behind the learnings presented in this book.

Eric Molale, Elias Magosi, Goaba Mosienyane, Gabaake Gabaake, the Botswana Police Service, the government of Botswana, and our many friends in this beautiful country – They have trusted us with aiding their transformational efforts for more than a decade.

The faculty and students at Texas Tech and the University of Alberta – For their support of our efforts in Botswana and for giving us time to write the book. A special thanks to Karen Patterson and Kim Boal for reading earlier drafts and to Roy Suddaby for listening to stories about wild dogs during many lunches.

Evelyn Hsu at the Maynard Academy and Laura Iturbide at Anahuac University for allowing us to "test drive" many pack leadership ideas in front of a live audience.

Bertrand Jouslin de Noray and our friends in the European Organization for Quality (EOQ) for sharing the discovery journey of transformation science.

Doug Beigel and COLA; Nancy Stueber and OMSI; Pricilla Cuddy and Leadership Oregon program – Teams of wild dogs moving the world forward.

Customer-Supplier Division of the American Society of Quality (ASQ) – Thank you for providing a platform for the emergence of several transformation concepts.

Paul O'Mara and Quality Press – Thank you for guiding this book through to publication.

And the utmost thanks to our families. – Marla, Jessica and Mark; Erika, Marvin Xavier and Miles Dakota. Without their love, patience, and support, none of this would have been possible.

1

The Best in Performance

KNOWLEDGE POINTS

- Leadership lessons can be found everywhere. We found some of those lessons in the wild while doing extensive work in Botswana and South Africa.

- Leadership is about leading, not about eating grass. A continual defensive posture yields little forward progress. Zebra-leaders and zebra-managers are quickly becoming extinct.

- Fast and decisive action by a leader can yield an advantage. Cheetah-leaders know the value of speed, but without the balancing skills to grow sustaining systems and develop a community of performers, they see success disappear as fast as it arrived.

- Lion-leaders understand power. The excessive and blatant wielding of power may be good for the ego, but the organization suffers. Emerging leaders tend to leave the lion-led organization in order to thrive.

- Wild dog leadership is the relentless pursuit of a clear vision, relying upon creativity, cohesiveness, and the strength of the pack. Wild dog leaders hold special insights about shared leadership, shared vision, tenacity, and strong individual contribution.

INTRODUCTION

We have a confession to make. We didn't go looking for the African wild-dog analogy as a way to describe our thoughts about effective leadership and high-performance teams. Rather, the analogy happened to find us. In this chapter, we describe how we came to develop leadership insights as a result of observing four animal survival styles, those of zebras, cheetahs, lions, and the African wild dog. We then outline the unique and successful hunting and socializing traits that characterize an effective leadership model.

LESSONS FROM THE ANIMAL KINGDOM

In our research work, study, and consulting, we have had the opportunity to travel the world and connect with wonderful leaders engaged in transforming their organizations. We wrote about this in a previous book titled *Transformational Leadership: Creating Organizations of Meaning.*[1] It is inspiring to see what spirit and sustained effort can produce, often in the face of limited resources.

For more than a decade, we have worked in South Africa, implementing performance management systems and conducting research with governments and with for-profit and non-governmental organizations.[2] In particular, we have held an enduring relationship

with the Botswana Public Service, both nationally and locally. It has been especially gratifying to witness the power of solid leadership in the face of numerous obstacles. Aiding this society in cultivating its organizational systems and leadership proficiency has been an honor.

During the time we spent there, we were able to see wildlife unique to Africa. By participating on safaris, game rides, and camp outings in the African bush country, we developed an appreciation for the wonders of our natural world. Africa in the wild is amazing. Seeing prey and predators in action gave rise to robust memories, and since we were heavily engaged in the study of leadership, lessons of the wild evolved into parallels with leadership practices.

ZEBRAS

On one particular trek into the African wild, we came upon a herd of zebras. When we inquired about their black and white stripes, the guide explained to us that each zebra has a unique pattern that is readily identified by other zebras. At birth, the mother often goes away from the herd in order to help the newborn focus on her pattern alone. A youngster born within the herd who fails to identify its mother faces potential fatal consequences, because only the mother will put forth the effort to nurture the young. The guide also told us that the stripes were for camouflage. Now, if you have ever been in the African wild, you know that the only animals you *can* see on the brown plains are the black and white zebras. Even so, the stripes of a zebra allow for an interesting defense.

To a herd of zebra wandering the wide open savannah in search of grass, the ability to see an approaching predator is critical, a matter of life and death. The herd acts as a sensing commune, with multiple ears and noses seeking dangerous noises and smells. When one zebra is startled into action, the whole herd responds.

Here is where the stripes come into the story. A zebra's stripes are not designed to disguise detection, as one understands the common usage of camouflage. Rather, they are designed to frustrate a predator. When zebras are chased, they stay within a herd formation, allowing their patterned bodies to overlap. This confuses the predator, which is instinctively programmed to select a single prey, attain focus, and attack. The individual zebra's identity is masked within the herd. The predator is confused, unable to determine where one zebra starts and another ends. In that split second of confusion often lies survival.

Zebras – Implications for Organizational Leadership

For zebras, the stripes are a wonderful defensive measure, but camouflage stripes do not represent a winning strategy for a vibrant organization. Blending in so as not to become a target is a poor substitute for bold leadership. When making sure that individuals are not picked off becomes the primary goal, when every person in authority avoids being singled out, the culture becomes suspicious and cautionary. Zebra-leaders appear to be in a distressed or resigned state of survival, trying to avoid the words of Donald Trump, "You're fired." Operating from a position of protectionism, activity may be heightened, but this style is insufficient to lead change. Zebra-minded leaders tend to hide in the crowd when times get tough or when retrenchment and labor reductions occur.

If the organization is in a holding pattern, slowly giving way to the world's forward progress, then being a zebra might be OK. Eating grass is fine if constancy or status quo is your primary purpose. Zebras are not bad or wrong, they are simply not leaders of change. Calm and contentment may be the desired state. Eating grass may be viewed as a standardization process, avoiding variation. Management of the grass-eating process may have a place in the organization, but it is not sufficient because the need to improve performance is ever present. Organizations may have had a need for grass-eating management in the past, but times have changed.

Societies and organizations have moved from needing optimizers of existing systems to needing broader participation by the organization in creating the future. Leadership is increasingly required at all levels. Management and leadership are both vital to ensuring individual performance and contribution. Great managers must also demonstrate leadership competencies in today's work world.

You may know several zebra-style employees. Where is the worst place for a zebra, in the front or the back of the herd? Of course, no one wants to be at the back. Those are the people most easily picked off, downsized, fired, or held back for poor performance. At the same time, while money, status, and promotion come with being in the front, many are not willing to embrace the perceived or real risks associated with that front position. The organization understands that being a leader can be a lonely business. The risks are real. Leaders are held accountable for decisions and mapping out the path forward. While there is comfort in being a zebra in the middle of the herd, especially when predators arrive, leaders must understand that when they raise their hands to lead, they stick out from the herd.

Zebra-minded leaders often have a well-developed sense of the organization and may quickly perceive out-of-the-ordinary signs indicating personal danger. Unfortunately, they may also be locked into the energy of the herd, running for cover and taking followers with them. The defensive posturing of the zebra-leader may then become the focus of the operational unit. Forward progress is slowed. Assuring that the leader is immune to blame becomes the unit's top priority, although never stated as such. Records are meticulously and painstakingly kept, in case accusations of poor performance arise. The defense is, "I obeyed the directive; I did as I was told." This protective stance is contrary to a focus on achieving results or giving birth to a broader outcome desired or required.

Leadership, however, becomes more and more about taking risks. The drive and the need to create the purposeful vision require a leader to step out in front. Taking on the risk of leadership flows from an impelling need to create the vision, a vision that necessitates leading others in the quest. Unfortunately, many people like the salary and status that comes along with being a leader, but shy away from the risks and dangers associated with leadership.

Learning all we can from zebras, our hunt for an effective leadership analogy drawn from the wild continues as we travel the African bush.

CHEETAHS

Cheetah *(Acinonyx jubatus)* means 'spotted one' in Hindi. Seeing a cheetah in the wild is an incredible experience. Sleek and muscular, these wild cats are astonishing in their acceleration and speed, and speed is their primary advantage on the savannah. As pointed out on a public broadcasting service television special:

> Most importantly, cheetah bodies are uniquely built for speed. Their small heads offer little wind resistance, while their exceptionally long legs allow them to take huge strides. During sprints, the cheetah spine acts like a giant spring, storing energy that can be released in explosive surges. The cheetah's enlarged heart, lungs, and liver help deliver bursts of oxygen and energy, while their specially ridged footpads help provide traction, much like a car's tire.[3]

The cheetah is the fastest of all land animals. It can accelerate from zero to 40 mph in three strides, a short two seconds! Full speed is slightly in excess of 70 mph. As the cheetah runs, only one foot at a time touches the ground. With its 20- to 25-foot stride, there are times when no feet are touching the ground.

The 'spotted one' approaches downwind of the prey, diminishing the distance prior to attack. Singling out an animal from the herd (possibly one of those zebras), the cheetah moves in with the stealth and

focus of a cruise missile. It waits, watches, and stalks. Finally it strikes with amazing speed, tripping up the back legs of its prey. It kills by clamping powerful jaws on the prey's throat. Often alone in its quest, the cheetah is self reliant but also limited in what it can accomplish as a solo actor.

When an attack occurs, the herd moves quickly, knowing that death is coming in at high speed. Maybe the cheetah will be successful, maybe not. The kill ratio is approximately three kills for every ten hunts. Regardless of whether the cheetah makes a kill or not, the herd will eventually reassemble in another spot virtually unchanged…and go back to eating grass. From afar, it would appear that nothing really changed. There may be one less animal in the herd, usually the slowest, weakest, and most isolated, but all seems to return to normal.

Cheetahs expend a tremendous amount of energy in making the kill. They may be so tired from the hunt that even when they win, sometimes they lose. This is because cheetah kills are a major source of food for lions. Knowing that the cheetah will be too tired to defend its reward, the lions wait until after the cheetah has made the kill and then effortlessly steal it.

Cheetahs – Implications for Organizational Leadership

In leadership, the cheetah-leader is vigorous is its attack of a single organizational issue at any one time. Seeking out the issue, the zesty cheetah-leader moves into action with the force and speed that are its predatory advantage. The lightning-fast strike provides drama and excitement. It is truly magnificent to see. Like a flash of energy, cheetah-leaders really know how to get the herd jumping. Leadership, yes! If only the organization would respond and change overnight, while the electricity is still in the air. But organizations, like herds, have predictable ways of beating this leadership style. More times than not, the herd simply moves away after a few individuals have had a close call and a terrible fright. As the cheetah tires, the organization returns to near normal conditions…grazing on the plains.

The cheetah-leader may or may not put the issue to rest. However, each person in the organization grasps the threat of being singled out as a part of the problem, and the organization scatters out of the way. The finger pointing begins, redirecting the cheetah-leader to a different person or department. Perhaps some regret sending a predator to colleagues, but it's better than being the target.

This quickness, focus, and speed may be directed against the critical issue and it may create some pain for a few. But whether or not anything is accomplished, the organization will regroup out on the water-cooler plain, looking much as it did before. Neglecting interdependency with other organizational systems and failing to address the systemic nature of complex problems often delivers ultimate failure. Passion blinds the cheetah to the need to take other hunters along on the journey. This puts responsibility for success in the hands of a single leader, banking on his or her energy and stamina, rather than harnessing the energy and passion of the organization as a whole.

If the organization rewards speedy, rash action with quick promotions, all is well with the cheetah-leader. Although abrupt interventions by this type of leader are only occasionally accompanied by lasting results, the promotion cycle has someone else in the seat by the time the organization returns to its natural state.

Watch out when you employ cheetah-leaders to do their work on the organization. Yes, they are sometimes useful to get things moving and knock down a critical barrier to success. But the characteristics of a cheetah-leader are often counter to the need for system-wide leadership, which is the essential ingredient of future success. A cheetah definitely looks like a leader, aggressive, quick, and decisive. But the results may tell a different story. A cheetah that goes on ten hunts comes back with a kill only three or four times…3/10…4/10. This is not a particularly remarkable level of performance effectiveness.

The cheetah study behind us, we continue our hunt for an effective leadership analogy in the wilds of Africa.

LIONS

What about the king of the animal kingdom…Leo, Simba, King of Beasts, the Wizard of Oz's beloved exemplar of courage, *Pantera leo*? What leadership lessons can we learn in the lion's approach to accomplishing its mission? This regal beast is much revered, and has occupied an honored and venerated position in literature throughout history. Powerful, courageous, and loyal, the lion deserves a look. Having seen a pride of fourteen quarreling over the meat of a small wart hog, we certainly have a profound respect for their combative skills as well as their appetites.

Covering hunting territories of up to 150 square miles, lions hunt in multiples.[4] In pairs or in large groups forming a broad front, lions prefer to go after large prey such as impalas, zebras, wildebeests, water buffalo, and giraffes. When times are tough, smaller animals will suffice. But for lions, who sleep up to 20 hours per day and who have the capacity to eat huge amounts of meat in one sitting, the bigger the

better. And they need a lot of food, with the males averaging 450 lbs. and the females 300 lbs. The lionesses does most of the hunting, while the males hang back with the cubs. Equipped with retractile claws and long canine teeth, their attack is ferocious. The best hunting occurs on moonless nights.

When food is available, the adult males have the first run at it. The term "lion's share" describes the gorging of meat by the males. After the males have had their fill, the cubs and the females, both hunters and non-hunters, fight over what remains.

The lion's social unit, known as a pride, ranges from a handful to as many as 40 animals. The collection of related females, their cubs, and one or two dominant males will cast off young maturing males, identified by the growing of a thick mane.[5] As young male cubs age, they are 'invited' to leave the pride. The older, dominant males do not need the competition.

The young adult males then make their own way, often traveling in smaller all-male groupings to aid in hunting efficiency. As they mature and grow in strength, a challenge to become the dominant male of an existing pride can result in a dramatic alteration of the pride. Infanticide often occurs as the newly dominant males strive to establish paternity within the pride. They kill young cubs and the subsequent births from already pregnant females.

Lions – Implications for Organizational Leadership

How can you recognize lion-leaders within an organization? First, they will stand out. Displaying dominance over the organizational pride, they will be the center of the community. Paternal in their protection of the community, lion-leaders will be loyal and will demand loyalty. When an acquisition occurs, the tendency will be to replace existing leaders (young cubs) with their own loyal associates. Results will flow, along with the blood.

Lion-leaders enjoy displaying their manes. Highly visible and wanting to be noticed, they have a large presence. Egos are at play. When lion-leaders take the time and energy from the mission at hand to stroke those egos, their organizations lose. They become a source of power drain, drawing off valuable energy from the accomplishment of critical corporate tasks. Jim Collins, author of *Good to Great*, speaks directly to this lion-leader trait and its liability in organizations:

> Fast Company: The CEOs who took their companies from good to great were largely anonymous. Is that an accident?
>
> Jim Collins: There is a direct relationship between the absence of celebrity and the presence of good-to-great results. Why? First, when you have a celebrity, the company turns into "the one genius with 1,000 helpers." It creates a sense that the whole thing is really about the CEO. At a deeper level, we found that for leaders to make something great, their ambition has to be for the greatness of the work and the company, rather than for themselves. That doesn't mean that they don't have an ego. It means that at each decision point—at each of the critical junctures when Choice A would favor their ego and Choice B would favor the company and the work—time and again the good-to-great leaders pick Choice B. Celebrity CEOs, at those same decision points, are more likely to favor self and ego over company and work.[6]

Strong emerging leadership is seen as a threat to lion-leaders. It is best to have promising new leaders leave the community when they are perceived to be a threat to the existing lion-leader. For example, recall that while Jeffrey Immelt won the chance to be the next CEO of General Electric (replacing Jack Welch), the other two internal CEO candidates actually left the company. A similar event occurred at Coca-Cola. The COO left when the company appointed someone else to be CEO. To do otherwise might be to have a budding leader encroach upon the existing dominant leader's drive to acquire the lion's share of credit, rewards, and recognition. In the wisdom of the lion-leader, it is prudent to avoid a future confrontation and battle for dominance. Off casting emerging competition accomplishes the objective of ego and territorial protection. Bright, hard-working producers do well in the organization...as long as they are subservient and dependent upon the lion-leader.

In such a lion-led organization, all goes well as long as the leader keeps the pride in check, remains strong, and makes sharp-witted strategic decisions. But any weakness by the lion-leader costs the pride heavily. The longevity of the organization is at risk...totally dependent upon the stamina and determination of the lion-leader. If the leader slips, all suffer because other potential leaders have been cast off.

The loyal followers have difficulty understanding any challenge to the lion-leader. In their eyes, success flows from the strength of the current leadership. Peace at any price is the mental mindset. When discord arises, Rodney King's voice can be heard: "Can't we just get along?" Internal conflict is seen as destructive and to be avoided. Indeed, the loyal followers are often part of the process of discarding emerging leaders who have differing opinions or approaches. All is well when everyone simply obeys the lion-leader, for he is the king of this jungle.

While lion-leaders are more promising than cheetahs and zebras, our search for a metaphor of leadership effectiveness continues on the savannah.

WILD DOGS OF AFRICA

Almost brought to extinction by the guns of ranchers protecting their livestock and other domestic animals, the wild dog of Africa (*lycaon pictus*, or "painted wolf" in Latin) is the most effective and successful hunter of all carnivores. While there is no clear standard of effectiveness in hunting, one estimate has the success of wild dogs at seven or eight kills on every ten hunts.[7] How are they so successful without the speed of the cheetah and the individual killing power of the lion? How does the wild dog hold the title for the most efficient hunter? According to McNutt and Boggs in their article *Running Wild: Dispelling the Myths of the African Wild Dogs:*

> Wild dogs have always impressed natural historians with their efficiency as communal predators and with their highly social behavior. The organization of wild dogs into packs, as is the case with many of the other canine species,

has been functionally related to the capturing of large prey relative to their body size. There is little doubt that hunting in a group facilitates the successful capture of relatively large prey, but social organization varies widely among canines and the causes underlying the extreme sociality reported for *Lycaon* (wild dogs) may be more complex than a functional explanation of one of its consequences.[8]

Living in packs ranging from two to thirty animals, wild dogs are led by a dominant male and female who serve as the alpha dogs. Their hunting strategy is to stalk and then pursue their prey until exhaustion overtakes the animal. In this way, a pack is able to kill large animals such as the wildebeest or kudu that can outrun the pack and easily dismiss individual dogs with deadly kicks. These animals work as a team to bring down prey many times their size. By tracking the prey and refusing to stop the chase, they run an animal to the point of collapse and then collectively bring it down. By their collective perseverance and tenacity, they achieve the goal.

We have witnessed firsthand the creativity of the wild dog. Nature reserves use electric fences to separate farm and range land from wildlife. Refusing to see electric fences as barriers, the dogs see them rather as an aid; they have become resourceful in taking down prey in this changing environment. A pack of dogs will herd their prey utilizing a strong initial hunt. They run antelope into the electric fence, temporarily stunning it. Once the prey falls, the wild dogs go for the kill. In this manner, they are able to take down large antelope in the shortest of time.

Working to build community does not mean the pack is void of confrontations, such as struggling to determine the "top dog." But the mission of taking down prey, and eating, is not compromised in the social dynamics. In fact, collective understanding exists that the community is the source of success. Research shows that operating with the principle of unity, combined with altruistic acts, is critical to the longevity of the pack:

> Recent research has shown the wild dog to have behaviors verging on classic altruism. This is particularly evident in pup rearing, which is a pack effort with males shouldering much of the responsibility. In fact in one instance, following the death of a pack female, male pack members were observed successfully raising her pups from the age of five weeks.

Perhaps the most obvious expression of the wild dogs' altruistic tendencies is their feeding style. After a prey animal has been successfully brought down, each pack member is allowed to eat. The feeding scene is a peaceful one rather than a savage frenzy. Disabled pack members share alongside more able adults, and pups receive regurgitated food from any adult in the pack. This behavior is uncharacteristic of other large carnivores, such as lions, which often fight over a carcass, jostling with each other for access to food.[9]

Wild dogs appear to hold long-term goals and to be able to envision the future. The considerable investment of time and energy is but the temporary cost to produce the vision. Perseverance and tenacity are their characteristics when it comes to the goal of killing a prey. Long hunts, up to three days, exhaust the prey, making it possible for the pack to take down the antelope without risking serious injury. If the dogs were to attack a large animal immediately, even in mass, antlers and hooves would inflict injury. By being patient and focused, the dogs chase the prey over long distances, attacking only when the prey is worn out. Success is achieved through doggedness.

Each dog must be engaged, showing up energetically and doing his part. Short-term performance dips and the maturation process are not penalized with death, but performance over time is expected. Each dog is required to perform. No performance, no food.

Having consulted numerous websites, books, and articles about wild dogs, we offer this paragraph to describe the reason for their greater success:

In this sense, pack mates (referring to a pack of wild dogs) often share in the capture of a single prey, but they do not co-operate or create strategies for hunting. Their hunting technique may more accurately be described as opportunistic, in the sense that they hunt as individuals with a common objective and respond opportunistically to changing conditions in the most effective way possible.[10]

We argue that the traits that make a pack of wild dogs an effective work team are shared leadership, shared vision, tenacity, and individual contribution. Following, we describe each in detail.

Pack Leadership

The unique thing about wild dogs is that, unlike lions, they exhibit pack leadership. All adult members are called upon to lead at one time or another, depending on their position in the hunt. Each pack includes an alpha, or dominant, male and female, who create the social order and who are allowed to breed. Their efforts are focused on bringing the community together as a pack, not on functioning as sole leaders of the hunt.

Typically, a hunt starts either early in the morning or late in the day. The older wild dogs usually start the hunt as they are often the hungriest. Once the wild dogs pick up the scent of an animal, they track it in a sort of relay fashion. They fan out along the plain and one animal leads the charge. If the prey changes direction, the wild dog closest to it becomes the leader for that part of the charge. They take turns on the attack, eventually wearing the animal down as described below:

> Wild dogs have a formation that they follow when hunting. It's always the furry ones that lead, and they stay in a line. When the front one gets tired, the next one takes over and the front one drops to the back of the line. That way they are always strong.[11]

It's interesting to note that, while they cooperate in the hunt, it is not a coordinated activity. There is no shared strategy or plan. Rather, the

wild dogs know the objective and they go for the kill. The opportunistic nature of the wild dog is a growing issue on game preserves. While a typical pack of wild dogs will take down an impala, rarely will they attack a water buffalo, zebra, or wildebeest; those animals are too big. However, on game preserves the animals are enclosed by an electric fence that keeps the lions and elephants in and the domesticated cattle out. Here the wild dogs have started running larger prey into the electric fence, where the shock stuns the prey long enough for the wild dogs to strike.

Pack Vision

While the wild dogs do not have an obvious leader, each pack clearly shares a similar vision. Wild dogs appear to instinctively know that the continual achievement of the pack vision is dependent upon the survival of the pack itself. This is not the case of lions, as illustrated below:

> Once the prey is dead, male lions, which are larger than the lionesses, chase away the females and eat first. After the males are finished eating, the females can feed, and then the cubs eat last. As a result, cubs often starve during periods of drought, when prey is scarce.[12]

When wild dogs make a kill, the youngest dogs eat first, then the dominant dogs, and finally the subordinate dogs. If the young eat the entire kill, the adults will simply hunt again. The dominant mother may be earlier to the feed table, but she is usually taking food to regurgitate for the babies she left behind. This order of eating does two important things. It allows the younger wild dogs to grow up strong, preparing them to be called upon in future hunts. It also keeps the subordinate wild dogs hungry, thereby providing motivation for the next day's hunt. The social dynamics within the pack ensure achievement of the pack vision over time.

Individual Contribution

Although wild dogs most often hunt in packs, this is not because they must in order to survive. Stories are told about wild dogs that exist by themselves for long periods. One story tells of a wild dog, tracked for more than eight months, that lived alone and made numerous impala kills. It appears that they join the pack not to strengthen the hunt, but to have company during the periods between hunts. Often new packs form when groups of siblings join another small group. Each dog is skillful as an individual contributor. The pack is composed of individual contributors, each adding significantly to the strength of the whole.

Tenacity

The last notable trait of wild dogs is tenacity. Unlike lions, whose hunting style revolves around overpowering their prey by means of surprise, speed, and power, wild dogs succeed because they never give up. Lions achieve their goals less often than the wild dogs. If the outcome of the hunt does not look favorable, if the circumstances are not advantageous to the lion's skill set, lions will stop hunting. Wild dogs, on the other hand, will pursue their prey for miles and for days, causing some to think the wild dog a cruel hunter. As the wild dog is much smaller than the lion and not as fast as the cheetah, its chief weapon is tenacity. Wild dogs simply wear down their prey. When the prey is in an exhausted state, the wild dogs move to the kill. In this way they are able to take down large prey, animals that at full strength could kill the dogs. This type of hunting is not as striking as the lion's fierce attack, or as demonstrative as the sleek speed of the cheetah. It is, however, highly effective.

ALPHA DOG – BRINGING THE PACK TOGETHER

Although all adult males display pack leadership traits, there are specific pack leaders…the female and male alpha dogs. They are in charge of social order and the pack forms around them as illustrated below:

> Just as the family dog may frequently solicit attention from its human pack members, so wild dogs beg attention from the dominant female. Dogs lick their master's faces; wild dogs lick at the mouth of the alpha animal, mimicking juvenile behavior that caused adults in the pack to regurgitate food. Dogs lie on their sides in submission, exposing their bellies for scratching; wild dogs indicate their position in the pack by similar body postures, exposing their throats and genitals to the dominant dog in attempts at appeasement. The dominant female lies on her side and allows the others in the pack to lick and nibble her body in a grooming ritual.[13]

The alpha dog of a modern organizational team brings the team together. She makes preparation for conscious, willful individuals to unite as a pack…a highly efficient and effective team. The alpha dog has a difficult task. Like the wild dogs of Africa, the team leader must have the stamina to pursue breakthrough change when the sun is shinning as well on dark, lonely nights when the spotlights are elsewhere. The alpha leader views each member of the pack as a skilled contributor in the present or in the near future. Each member is a spirit full of energy and creativity. Bringing this energy together, while insisting upon individual contribution, is a dance. Faced with challenges, team leaders may revert to lion-leadership or cheetah-leadership characteristics, thus sub-optimizing the strength of the group.

Wild dog alpha leaders have the competence to lead with vision, the wherewithal to enroll and energize others to achieve a living vision and to address unexpected barriers along the way. These leaders move the organization forward. Leadership is often said to be of the spirit; the alpha leader has a spirit devoted to producing an exceptional pack of wild dogs…wild dogs that will create greatness within the organization.

The alpha leader is also good at managing the team. Drawing a distinction, great managers organize the current, known assets and resources to deliver upon the present mission of the organization. Skillful in the areas of analysis and administration, they are energetic in their work and they demonstrate high individual performance. It is said that management is of the mind, intellect, and hard work combined.

An alpha leader who demonstrated strong leadership characteristics, including the managerial skills, was Dick Winters. His story and leadership successes were made famous in Stephen Ambrose's *Band of Brothers*, the epic World War II story of Easy Company, 506th Parachute Infantry Regiment, 101st Airborne Division. In his book *Beyond the Band of Brothers*, Winters speaks strongly about leading from the front:

> "You cannot make sound decisions unless you are at the point of attack. Leaders should always position themselves where the critical decision must be made. Precisely where that location should be is a judgment call, but in my experience leaders should be as far forward as possible. Successful leaders must be highly visible, if for no other reason than to share the hardships of their men."[14]

In his leadership of Easy Company, Winters demonstrated the skills of delegation and shared leadership. These are not in conflict with leading from the front. Winters' own physical development and mental development were instrumental in his effectiveness, allowing him to display individual performance and personal contribution in executing alpha dog leadership.

Alpha leaders are skilled in leading while having suitable management expertise. But their skills also include the forming of pack vision, empowering team members, employing creativity, and building community. We will look at the alpha leader in more detail in chapter six, but first we will further investigate the defining wild dog characteristics of pack leadership and pack vision. The traits of tenacity and individual contribution will be covered in chapter four; how to form a pack is the topic of chapter five.

ANALOGIES AND UNDERSTANDING COMPLEX PROCESSES

In the thorny arena of understanding and exploring new leadership approaches, comparisons with simple, working examples can be helpful. Seeing rough equivalence between two circumstances or operations holds the possibility for new insights. For example, the automobile was initially known as a horseless carriage. The term provided a helpful comparison, bringing into the mind's eye something that was well known, a carriage, but with a twist…a self-powered carriage.

Be aware that similarities do not hold in every aspect of an analogy, and herein lies the danger. Where comparisons may hold certain insights in one regard, dissimilarities are overlooked at a cost. Yes, an automobile has four wheels and provides transportation, much like a carriage. But it wasn't the absence of the horse that made the automobile move forward in history. The combustion engine is not addressed in the concept of the horseless carriage, and this dissimilarity is a key component of the automobile.

So, analogies can be useful to a point, but only to stimulate the brain to look at alternatives in understanding complexity. Use them to kick start your mental engine, encouraging agility of the mind. We understand that often analogies produce more questions than answers. In the case of the wild dog analogy, you might be asking why the kill rate is an appropriate measure of success. Perhaps the cheetah and lion kill less because they kill bigger game. Or, if the wild dog is so successful, why are they almost extinct? While these are good questions, we think they distract from the basic point of the book. Our basic point is that new leadership approaches are developing and we think that the analogy of the wild dog will help leaders, managers, and individuals in society understand these new approaches. It's not that the world no longer needs zebras, cheetahs, and lions (both the animals themselves and the types of people they represent). Later in the book we address this in more detail. For now, let's explore how you can change your leadership style to incorporate insights from the wild dogs!

Action Opportunities

- Take the leadership test in Appendix A. Note your strengths and weaknesses. Lions and cheetahs typically score high on Performer and Energetic. Wild dogs score high on Vision, Creativity, and Community Builder. We will go into more detail on this test in Chapter 6.

NOTES

1. Stephen Hacker and Tammy Roberts, *Transformational Leadership: Creating Organizations of Meaning* (Milwaukee: Quality Press, 2005).
2. Our results of this study can be found in *Leadership and Organization Development* 26 (5) 400-411, *Public Service Management Journal,* and *Measuring Business Excellence,* 8 (3): 52-59
3. *PBS's nature: Cheetahs in a Hot Spot.* http://www.pbs.org/wnet/nature/cheetahs/hunters.html
4. IUCN, The World Conservation Union, Cat Specialist Group, 1996 http://lynx.uio.no/catfolk/afrleo02.htm
5. The Cyber Zoomobile. http://home.globalcrossing.net/~brendel/lion.html
6. Collins, Jim; *Fast Company,* Issue 51, October 2001, page 90. http://www.fastcompany.com/online/51/goodtogreat.html
7. John McNutt and Leslie Boggs *Running Wild: Dispelling the Myths of the African Wild Dogs* (Smithsonian Books, 1997).
8. (McNutt and Boggs, 1996: 7)
9. Conservation Spotlight: Wild Dogs. Excerpted from S. Rotz Mamakos, *AZA Communiqué, Dec. 1996* http://www.umich.edu/~esupdate/library/97.01-02/mamakos.html
10. (McNutt and Boggs, 1996; 70-71)
11. (McNutt and Boggs, 1996: 70)
12. (http://www.dtngroup.com/sdkids/kids/animals/lions)
13. Woolf, Norma Bennett; http://www.canismajor.com/dog/afriwild.html
14. Dick Winters, *Beyond the Band of Brothers.* (New York, Penguin Group, 2006).

2

Leadership Journey

KNOWLEDGE POINTS

- Understanding leadership is an ongoing process as social, technological, and societal forces continue to alter the organizational landscape.

- Contextual shifts and increased performance requirements cause an evolution in leadership methods and strategies.

- The Leadership Development Cycle offers a path to conscious development of skills.

- Analogies allow a grasp of complex concepts in a non-linear fashion...but, although powerful, their effectiveness is limited.

INTRODUCTION

Now that you have read about a new approach to successful leadership, the concept of the alpha dog and a pack of wild dogs, the question remains. "Now what?" Our answer is that now you have the opportunity to change, enhance, and develop a more effective leadership style. Leadership is not a stagnant subject. As human civilization develops, leadership advances and matures in its approach. Even a brief look back into history speaks to this progression. Attila the Hun may have been right for the early fifth century, but another style was needed when Mahatma Gandhi took the lead to free India from British rule. Napoleon was called upon to strengthen France, but this leadership style would have been inappropriate for John F. Kennedy during the Cold War. Times change and so do the characteristics of an effective leader. The world stage, the context in which a leader operates, is dynamic. The performance expectations of leaders evolve.

THE CONTEXT OF LEADERSHIP IS DYNAMIC

As society, organizations, and individuals change and transform, the need for leadership to adjust and modify its approach becomes evident. Take a look at changes that have happened in just the past twenty years. Information, once the guarded treasure of leaders, is now found in abundance on the web and in print. Financial disclosures, executive compensation, independent performance trends of products and services, and governmental agency performance stats are widely available in today's information age. Future employment trends, hot areas for technology growth, and world market analysis are accessible. Once sheltered from holding a leadership view, followers can now discover and form an accurate picture of the environment in which a particular organization is operating, its financial health, and public sentiment about it. The leader is no longer the only one privy to this critical information.

Because of this increase in the amount and availability of information, the function of leadership must shift or expire. Possibly painful for some, yet each leader must answer the value-added question, "If I am no longer the sole provider of critical business information, what do I bring to the organization that is unique?" Successful leaders have moved to emphasize vision, analytical skills, and boundary management. With information now widely available, the thriving leaders interpret the information in light of a compelling vision and build the case for productive change. They recognize how to create the compelling story of the future of the organization in part by listening, validating, and leveraging the information brought forward by followers.

At one time in our history, the ideal leader was thought to be the best performer. He or she was thought to be the "all-knowing person" who understood the work of the organization in great detail. For example, consider the World War I submarine captain. Trained to understand the workings of the entire submarine and often the source of problem-solving knowledge, the captain had exceptional skill and familiarity with each working station. By World War II, submarines had become more technically complicated instruments of war; the captain was still expected to have tremendous knowledge and operating skills for each station. At this time adherence to Navy protocol relaxed; crew members were allowed to interact with the captain in an environment that supported learning. Problem solving was accomplished in a more cooperative and participatory manner. The captain still had the last word, but sharing knowledge from a number of sources, including the each sailor's abundant work-station knowledge, was more common. The ability to harness that knowledge became the new leadership skill called empowerment.

Now the world has the ballistic submarine of the twenty-first century. It would take multiple lifetimes to train a captain of today's modern attack submarines with the problem-solving skills needed to address every possible predicament or crisis aboard these nuclear vessels. The role of the captain has shifted. Much more strategic in his or her thinking, today's captain relies heavily upon the crew's knowledge of individual working stations. This idea is beautifully summed up in the exchange between Gene Hackman and Denzel Washington in the movie *Crimson Tide*. Gene Hackman, the old leader, is challenged by Denzel Washington, Hackman's second in command. In a heated discussion, Hackman tells Washington, "When I got my command, they gave me a target packet and a button to push and told me when to push it. Now they seem to want you to know why."

Leaders of high-tech organizations aren't required to know every aspect of their operations. Instead, they are called upon to align human resources, to provide inspiration through market competence, and to have high levels of emotional intelligence rather than exceptional technical competence.

In addition to information and technical shifts, the broad application of high-performance work systems has blurred the line between worker, manager, and leader. Downsizing has brought increased responsibilities to the average worker coupled with the need for critical cross-functional skills. Today's worker is more involved in the decisions of the organization. Today's leader is faced with a very different workforce than in the past. The resulting requirements for leadership have shifted once again.

Global sourcing, remote workforces, fluid partnership-building organizations, sharp technological shifts, and rapid-innovation-driven product and service lines combine to determine the most effective manner in which to lead. We find examples of these transformative forces in stock brokerage firms, not-for-profits, international businesses, U.S. armed services, and government service. Leadership in these types of organizations has shifted and adjusted to the context changes. Since the changes in our organizational world keep on coming, leadership must continue to transform in order to be effective.

Performance Requires Advancements in Leadership

Another reason for the continuous study of leadership is that the performance bar continues to rise. All types of organizations are asked to do more with less, at a faster pace and with higher quality. Competition abounds. Appointment committees, boards of directors, and organizational heads demand higher leadership performance to meet the overall organizational goals and to keep the entity afloat. Less tolerance for faltering leadership is present and faster ramp-up times are now the norm. From CEOs to government leaders, the risk of dismissal looms heavily.

In the sports world, this is also visible. As we were writing this text, Ron Zook, the head coach of the University of Florida's football team, was fired. He had the best record of any second-year coach of a college team (16 victories and 2 losses). He took the school to two post-season bowl games. By all accounts, he had the best recruiting class with more high school all-Americans committing than any other year at Florida since 1987. Yet he was fired because the University of Florida expected more.

With the increased performance expectations of leadership, rewards flow to producers. Salaries have leaped for proven leaders. The dizzying escalation of top leadership compensation packages is astounding. With the rising rewards, immediate results are demanded in return, even in difficult situations. In some cases, these compensation packages are now being disputed by persons outside the boardrooms. Dick Grasso was awarded tens of millions in deferred compensation while leading the New York Stock Exchange. Many think his outstanding performance should have come at a cheaper price. What was seen as remarkable leadership performance at one time appears to have moved to a commodity status.

The hesitance to engage in the ongoing study of leadership may come from fatigue in meeting the ever-increasing demands on performance. These demands are consistently raised. No longer are leaders required simply to win the war, introduce new products, cross the Red Sea, or win a championship. New leaders are tasked with winning multiple wars, managing the troops during peace time, and feeding the followers who crossed the Red Sea, all while attaining multiple championships. Anxiety concerning personal leadership performance may come to the surface. The angst related to reading 'yet another leadership book' comes from fear of finding deficiencies in personal style or approach...and uncovering yet another area to develop. Many leaders feel more in the spotlight than ever. What worked for them in the past simply is insufficient in today's world. The quest to learn more about their trade as leaders is brought front and center.

Justified or not, breakthrough performance by leaders in our top organizations means that other organizations must follow suit. When that performance becomes widely known, the life of the organization itself depends upon better performance. If the organization fails to respond to the improvements of competitive organizations, it dies. Organizations, governments, and sports dynasties die everyday. Where are the Roman and the Ottoman Empires? How many championships have the Boston Celtics (of the National Basketball Association) or the San Francisco 49ers (of the National Football League) won lately? What happened to Montgomery Ward? What is currently happening with Sears and Ford?

LEADERSHIP LEARNING CYCLE

To gain insight into emerging leadership requirements, an ongoing learning stance is needed...learning about leadership itself. But before people can develop leadership skills, they must develop self mastery. Self mastery is the understanding of personal skills, assets, gifts, talents, and abilities. Self mastery is also the awareness of potential development opportunities. A first step towards self mastery is self awareness. Great performers have a strong awareness of self. They know why they exist and where they are going. Great performers realize the need to continually develop skills that will get them to where they wish to go. Be it Tiger Woods developing a new swing to make him a better golfer or Michael Jordan moving from slasher and slam-dunker to jump shooter to make him a better basketball player, great performers develop the necessary skills to take them there. They are vision and goal focused. Talented leaders keep on learning. The study of leadership is a never-ending commission. As the environment shifts, the flourishing leader takes time to study individual effectiveness and translates those lessons into performance excellence for the organization.

Employing the concept of a learning stance can be helpful for individuals who want to improve their self mastery and their leadership skills. Based upon a modification of the development cycle by Dr. W. A. Shewhart of Bell Laboratories, seeing leadership development within a Plan-Do-Study-Act cycle offers assistance. Understood within a development cycle, it becomes clear that leadership development is not just an academic study. In other words, acquiring intellectual knowledge is not an end in itself. Rather, it is a component designed to improve the performance of active leadership.

The leadership development cycle (Figure 2.1) can be of value in understanding the role of intellectual knowledge. Beginning with creating a leadership plan (gathering knowledge, creating self-awareness through assessment, making personal strategic choices) a leader chooses to take on a leadership challenge. The mindset is one of choice rather than a feeling of coercion into a leadership role. Leadership is a choice to move toward a real, tangible vision…a vision connected to the leader's life purpose. A reluctant leader is rarely an effective leader.

Leadership is a unique calling. The call itself flows from a defined purpose…a reason for being. Answering the question "Why are you here; why are you in this life?" can be difficult, but the rewards are great. Developing consciousness concerning your existence aids in the creation of a vision. From that vision, the leadership call comes into play. Not all purposes and visions require substantial leadership. For instance, if your purpose is to help alleviate human suffering using your personal medical skills, then you could make an individual contribution as a medical surgeon. However, if your vision includes the creation of a superior medical staff, leadership qualities are required and leadership becomes a calling for creating the vision.

Leadership Development Cycle

FIGURE 2.1   Leadership development cycle.

Getting clarity on the vision is the easy part; the true challenge comes with actually leading. With the actions of leadership come results. Successes and failures follow. Some results are met with approving inner smiles; other results are greeted with self criticisms. From here, a leader begins the process of studying the results. What are the key lessons flowing from the leadership experience? What deserves to be repeated and standardized? What traits or characteristics must be altered? The study of personal and collective leadership performance guides growth in leadership effectiveness. The beauty of leadership experience is that both failures and successes have the potential to contribute lessons. The denial of failures cuts off the leader from a rich source of learning. A cursory review of great leaders will quickly point to their capitalizing on the wisdom of past failures.

Environmental feedback is a primary source of data for making a leadership study. What does the environment (followers, customers, advocates, and detractors) have to say about your leadership effectiveness? A complete, 360-degree scan of the environment means seeking input from all surrounding sources—superiors, peers, subordinates, customers, and suppliers. This feedback, coupled with a look at the measurable progress toward attaining the stated vision and an abundance of data, is available for use in the study phase.

The final phase of the development cycle is to standardize and act upon the lessons derived from the study phase. This entails making the corrections necessary to attain enhanced performance. Leaders avoid the destructive stubbornness of having to be 'right' about past decisions, which reduces the risk of knowingly forging ahead in a futile direction. When protecting the ego supplants the stated vision, poor decisions of the past are not acknowledged. This leads to continual failure. Recognize mistakes and make the needed course correction.

Standardizing change is part of this step in the Leadership Development Cycle. At this point, the changes that were needed and made become part of continuous improvement. Losing weight, for example, is an improvement initiative. Keeping the weight off is the standardization of that improvement. The important thing is to use leadership lessons and insights to form new habits.

Self-mastery entails understanding. History shows that increased understanding can arise from the process of reflection. As straightforward as the Leadership Development Cycle has proven to be, the tendency is strong to jump into a leadership position and give it a go, to learn on the job. Reflection is deferred for another time and the study of leadership results is put aside. This failure to take time to think, to examine the leadership lesson, leads down a dangerous and difficult path.

A number of great leaders had reflection time forced upon them in the form of prison sentences. These leaders spent time reflecting on the results they created and determining how to further improve their leadership upon release from prison. Martin Luther King, Jr., Nelson Mandela, Cesar Chavez, Mahatma Gandhi, Adolph Hitler, Fidel Castro, and the Apostle Paul served time in prison, where they considered past results and pondered future, post-prison actions. Short of spending time in prison, aspiring leaders must take time out of a crisis-ridden schedule to think and reflect. This will certainly benefit a leader seeking to grow in effectiveness.

As new insights come during the reading of this text, the opportunity before you is to put into practice the knowledge you've gained. Experiment with differing approaches based upon solid modeling. See what the results may be. Standardize, make routine, the leadership actions that bring positive results and discard those with unsatisfactory outcomes.

Action Opportunities

- Become a life-long learner of leadership. Set measurable monthly reading goals in order to advance your knowledge base. Along with subject-specific texts, biographies are an excellent source of learning. One of the greatest leaders we know reads 52 books a year as part of his plan for leadership effectiveness.

- Experiment with leadership techniques. Standardization has its place in cementing powerful leadership traits, but without experimentation, you'll be left behind.

- Take some "prison time." Use the Leadership Development Cycle to carve out time for reflection.

- Find a feedback coach, someone in your organization who you trust to give open, honest, and direct feedback about your performance and your abilities.

3

Individual Traits of the African Wild Dog

KNOWLEDGE POINTS

- A pack of wild dogs is composed of strong and valued individual contributors.

- Individual contributors are tenacious and authentic and have the requisite skills for the task at hand.

- It's necessary to create a vision with clarity, commitment, and conviction in order to ensure the crucial characteristic of tenacity.

INTRODUCTION

This wild dog analogy for effective leadership and leadership teams is not just our invention. A wealth of academic and practitioner research has concluded that the wild dog traits of pack vision, pack leadership, tenacity, and individual contribution produce effective leadership teams (Figure 3.1).

In the next two chapters, we go into more detail on these four traits. In this chapter, we examine the traits of tenacity and individual contribution. As part of a high-performance team, each member's contribution is critical to fulfilling the resource utilization criteria. The trait of tenacity speaks to the results orientation aspect of a high-performance team. Other characteristics of a high-performance team exist within the wild dog team, but they are not distinctive in nature.

Wild Dog Teams

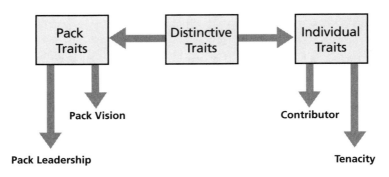

FIGURE 3.1 Wild dog teams.

INDIVIDUAL CONTRIBUTION

Given the eager interdependence demonstrated by the pack, individual contribution would seem to take a back seat. However, this is not the case. Individual contribution is essential for creating a truly powerful wild dog team. It is a case of having both interdependent performance (relationship or people mastery) *and* high individual contribution.

Contribution is precisely what is demanded of successful teams, and individual results are necessary to ensure team success. And what is the role of individual skill? Individual skill is a platform for worthy contribution, but skill alone is not sufficient. Too often skillful people fail to contribute, driven by various reasons. While *skill* speaks to demonstrated potential, *contribution* represents actual constructive action toward an objective.

Complicating matters is the relationship between the individual contributor and the need for teamwork in order to generate success. As with a high-performance sports team, individual contribution is a prerequisite to greatness, but having celebrated players alone does not guarantee success. Both individual contribution and interpersonal mastery are indispensable in achieving world-class status. The phrase 'dream team' usually denotes a team of highly accomplished individuals, but history is full of collections of great individuals that do not equal great teams.

The USA 2004 Olympic men's basketball team was thought to be another dream team, destined to sweep the competition and grab the gold. But dream teams are not always winners. During the initial matches, the USA men's basketball team, all great individual players, displayed a level of team performance on the court that was disappointing at best...bordering on embarrassing. As a collection of world-class players, they lacked world class team skills...possibly because the Olympic team included players from several standing NBA teams. Only after some competitive play time did the dream team start to perform as a team. Squeezing into the quarter finals, they came together to produce a medal. Sometimes the missing ingredient of a first-rate team is, ironically, teamwork. Superior athletes coupled with exceptional teamwork drive success. Amazingly, the USA basketball team produced similar results in the 2006 Olympic qualifying tournament.

Wild dog teams do not downplay individual contribution in order to bolster the case for teamwork. In fact, the celebration of individual contribution is commonplace. Often heard is the expression, "There is no *I* in the word *team*." Well, there may be no *I* in *team*, but there certainly is an *I* in *high-performance team*. Wild dog teams understand the need for both individual contribution and teamwork.

Often great individuals who fail at being a team resemble cheetahs, each doing his own thing. Relying on their individual gifts, team members rush in and make a stir. As with the cheetah and its advantageous speed, they sometimes make a kill. But because the benefits of teamwork are not well understood, a team of exceptional contributors may end up just moving the problems around without achieving long-term success. Cheetah-leaders may feel proud of their individual performance and cast the blame for failure on the team itself. What a counter example of leadership!

Also possible, highly competent individuals who lack trust for each other may end up looking like a pride of lions. Although accurate in their individual self assessments, the powerful egos and a generous dose of mistrust poison the team's performance. The team or corporate objective fades as self promotion rises. Given the number of strong individual contributors, conflicts easily arise as the win-lose game of ego superiority is in play. In short, not only do successful teams require successful individuals, the individuals must commit themselves to operating within a team.

It appears that the African wild dogs place great trust in all members of the group. A pack of wild dogs recognizes that each must contribute at the highest level in order for the group to be successful. In short, wild dogs seem to understand that while one might do more of the work, that one will not get more of the rewards; that would be lion thinking.

In nature, wild dogs have a deep sense of their individual contributions. Each dog has a role and is expected to fulfill that role with excellence. Only a portion of the pack will go on a hunt while others stay behind as protection for the young, who are easy targets. It's interesting to note that wild dogs often take turns feeding the young. In fact, feeding is approached as somewhat of a corporate responsibility seized by individual dogs. The specific tasks undertaken by each dog are not driven by ego but by an authentic assessment of abilities to fill critical roles. Both individual contribution and social/team performance are found in the pack. The strongest dogs go on the hunt; the dogs that are the best protectors stay back. No job is taken because it is more glamorous than another.

Members of wild dog organizational teams have high awareness of individual skills and hone these skills to near perfection. They readily recognize individual contribution as well as team success. As contrasted with the 2004 Olympic men's basketball team, bring to mind the 2004 Olympic USA women's basketball team...a true gold medal team. Clearly, the team required individual performance but also understood the role of interpersonal mastery, both on and off the field. Supportive in nature, they saw their prey, the gold, and marched forward. The women's team worked on their individual and their team skills. The women's team practiced together for six months, whereas the men's team only practiced together for about three weeks. The women's team played 13 games together before they started the Olympic competition; the men only played 6 games prior to the Olympics.

In business, this same wild dog pack behavior can be seen in exceptional product teams. Diversity of skills is appreciated for the various contributions it brings forth. Team members, each a valuable contributor with different life experiences, professional talents, and abilities, can produce a competitive edge if they remain focused on a single mission.

The responsibility to hone individual skills resides primarily with the individual. In annual work plans, for example, skill building should be outlined. Concentrating on the development of meaningful skills in order to produce superior individual performance is an ongoing obligation. This performance must be cast in the light of the team's vision—the pack's vision—in order to be relevant.

TENACITY

Another important characteristic of wild dogs is their tenacity. This trait separates wild dogs from other predators. Wild dogs hunt until their prey becomes exhausted and can no longer run away. Determination is the secret ingredient., Keeping the prey as the focal point and not giving into exhaustion ensures the meal.

As human's we often don't want it to be that simple, but great performance requires tenacity. As Kenyans dominate the world of long distance running, experts and lay-people alike want the answer to be found in their genetics, or in their diets, or with Kenya's altitude. Maybe the answer is simply that the Kenyans run more miles at faster speeds. In *Runner's World* Magazine, they describe their running this way: In the morning they run 10K, in the afternoon they run 15K, at night they might run an additional 10K, and then they do it all again the next day. The recent success of Vijay Singh in golf is another example. Why is he so good? Maybe it is because he just practices harder. While the other contenders to Tiger Woods' golfing throne are looking for excuses, Vijay goes to the practice range and hits more balls.

Popular literature about teams and groups can be misleading. Numerous articles detail how quality programs, financial tools, information systems, and communication methodologies can lead to team and organizational success. However, while these tools might help, they are not the guaranteed "quick fix." The right tools combined with inadequate persistence will not yield results. But an abundance of tenacity, even with poor tools, will eventually yield observable results. Do superior tools provide an advantage? Yes! But they do not secure performance. When faced with a choice between abundant resources and few resources coupled with an insatiable hunger for results, choose the few.

In *Leading Change: Why Transformation Efforts Fail*, the author describes eight reasons why change efforts fall short. Three of these reasons deal with tenacity (or lack thereof): not communicating the vision; not removing the barriers to achieving the vision; and declaring victory too soon. Missing is the tenacity of the individuals in the organization to persevere. Often in an organization, the team discards a tool that does not produce the desired effect quickly enough and then goes in search of another tool or technique. Wild dog teams, on the other hand, pursue their objectives with the tools they have, backed by the commitment to apply whatever time and energy is required. Groups could benefit from incorporating the same strategies.

The ability to hold on, not giving way to doubt or fatigue, is a wild dog team characteristic. Perseverance through rough times is rooted in the belief that a wise choice has been made and that the execution of the tasks ahead will determine success. All that must be done is to stay the course and complete the mission.

ROLE OF PACK VISION IN EMPLOYING TENACITY

In the next chapter we will discuss in more detail the pack traits of vision and leadership, but a note is needed here regarding the link between pack vision and individual tenacity. This link is important. If the vision fails to be deep rooted, lacking clarity, commitment, and conviction, doubt may set in when times get tough. Questioning the pack vision in times of stress destroys energy and focus. While on a difficult hunt for a team objective, being able to rely upon the firmness of the vision is critical.

Clarity of pack vision is essential. Is the pack vision multi-sensational? In other words, can pack members taste, feel, see, hear and smell the vision? For example, think of a simple lunch buffet. The words fall short of invoking strong desire. Now, start to describe actual dishes, the dining environment, and the social context. Envision the starched table cloth, the aromatic dishes, and the lively conversation. The vision grows in strength. A clear organizational vision taps upon the same multi-sensational strength. The feel of success, the taste of victory, and the smell of accomplishment are born out of real sensations, not just poetry. What constitutes the trumpeting of accomplishment in the sought-out vision? Spending time in holistic visioning of success is worthwhile.

Ample commitment to the pack vision emerges when an individual has a developed life vision and sees a connection to the pack vision. Having the self awareness of one's purpose allows a matching process to occur with respect to the pack vision. For individuals who are unsure, who have never questioned why they exist or in what direction they are traveling, the pack vision may hold attraction. It is, at least, an answer. But the root structure is shallow. In the most effective cult indoctrinations, the objective is to supply the answers to life without the individual's spirit taking part. Providing all the answers to the vulnerable candidate, the cult programs the individual with the hardwiring of cult reasoning and cult thinking. Resistance to this programming is found in individual purpose and belief systems....individual spirit. The weakness of a cult appears when individuals start to think on their own. Be it Jim Jones, Heaven's Gate, or the Nazi SS, cults are susceptible to individual spirit.

A stronger source of energy is discovered when the pack purpose and vision are found to be in alignment with individual purpose and vision. It's desirable that individual pack members know who they are and where they are going. Volunteering this life spirit in conjunction with other pack members toward a common vision produces robust commitment. Being conscious of individual spirit is the backbone needed to build a robust collective consciousness and the ensuing pack vision.

Conviction implies the rightness of the vision. The pack vision is true, fitting, and suitable. It rings of truth, as understood by the individual pack member. It is the right vision, given the context of personal and collective desire. The vision has been thought through and is fortified by the deep-seated knowledge of personal values and operating principles. Regardless of the positions of other teams or organizations, the chosen vision is as it should be for this team and for each of this team's members.

When the vision is clear, commitment strong, and conviction inherent, then the strength to carry the vision to completion is present. Wild dog teams take the time to develop the vision, understanding that its muscle is directly tied to the tenacity of each member and that dogged effort will be required in order to accomplish great visions.

WILD DOG CASE STUDY #1:
EARNEST SHACKLETON AND
THE ENDURANCE EXPEDITION

Imagine it is 1914. You're trapped on an iceberg eight hundred miles from the nearest civilization. By now you have abandoned your plan to be among the first explorers to cross the South Pole and your thoughts turn to survival. How will you survive? You have only a small life boat capable of carrying six crew members. Given the strong winds and currents, one wrong navigational error and you miss your target island. This was the fate surrounding the Endurance mission led by Earnest Shackleton. While most stories paint Shackleton as the hero and leader of the organization, this expedition was a classic case of wild dog accomplishment.

In 1914, Shackleton and 29 other men, many of whom had traveled with him on previous adventures, embarked on a courageous mission. Almost immediately, they were faced with danger in the form of ice that froze around them and trapped their boat. Engineering a heroic plan, they traveled to Elephant Island. Twenty-three men stayed behind while six men, led by Shackleton, made the daring boat journey to Georgia Island. Not only did the six men arrive at Georgia Island, they returned to Elephant Island some four months later to rescue the other twenty-three.

While many, including the author of *Shackleton's Way: Leadership Lessons from the Great Antarctic Explorer,* consider this a story of Shackleton's great leadership ability, we suggest that this story is more about the triumphs of pack leadership. True, Shackleton did display great "alpha dog" traits. He used many different skills to keep the twenty-eight other men safe, sane, and healthy during their more than two-year journey. A deeper look shows other pack traits.

The first trait is obvious but worth stating. The pack had to change its goals. Their first goal was to cross the South Pole; facing immediate danger, they switched to the goal of saving the lives of all their men. This was no simple feat. Shackleton sent another expedition to the other side of the South Pole to leave rations for them, which meant that his men had to carry only enough food and supplies for about three-fourths of the trip. That crew lost two men due to the harsh environment. Sir Edmund Hillary, in his introduction to F. A. Worsley's book version of the story (Worsley was the captain of the ship), called this the most amazing exploration story.

The second obvious trait is that of tenacity. Here is where Edmund Hillary writes it best: "Danger is one thing, but danger plus extreme discomfort for long periods is quite another. Most people can put up with a bit of danger—it adds something to the challenge—but no one likes discomfort—or not for long anyway." For two years they wore the same clothes, never able to take them off due to the cold. They were all alone with no other human contact. They had no idea if they would get home. The world had assumed that all had died and no one was trying to save them. What kept them going was the need to keep going.

With tenacity came strong shared leadership. Shackleton was a great leader, Frank Wild a great second in command, and Frank Worsley a great captain. While Shackleton conceived the plan, it was Wild who remained with the twenty-two men on Elephant Island for four months. It was Worsley who actually navigated the boat from Elephant Island to Georgia Island, a trip of more than 800 miles. The amazing feat could only be accomplished because these three men had the deepest level of trust, faith, and commitment to each other and to their respective missions—lead the team, navigate their position in the rough water by the light of the moon, and keep the other twenty-two men alive.

If we look below the 'obvious glow of leadership,' we see a pack of wild dogs that gave everything they had to a changed goal. Gone were thoughts of crossing the South Pole; now they were focused on returning home with everyone alive.

Action Opportunities

- What are the critical skills you offer a team and what contributions can you make?

- Why are you here on earth? What is your life purpose or reason for being? What is your individual vision of the future, say three years out? Can you envision the specific results you will have achieved?

- Where have you demonstrated tenacity? What was behind your persistent application of energy to accomplish this goal?

- Is your team's vision clear, evoking commitment and conviction?

4

Uniqueness of Pack Orientation

KNOWLEDGE POINTS

- A pack is a unique type of team. A team is but a particular form of community.

- There are two distinct pack traits that lead to wild dog performance: pack vision and pack leadership.

- Pack vision is a movement toward community building.

- Pack leadership is a recognition that, in order for the community to be successful, leadership must come from many members, not just from the alpha males and females.

INTRODUCTION

In the previous chapters we provided the foundation for understanding a new concept of leadership, specifically that of a pack of wild dogs. First we made the performance case. Wild dogs make a kill eight times out of ten. Lions and cheetahs are closer to four kills out of ten attempts. Then we described some of the reasons for their success: pack leadership, pack vision, individual skill, and tenacity. In this chapter we expand upon the pack traits of leadership and vision, but first we define the concept of the pack (Figure 4.1).

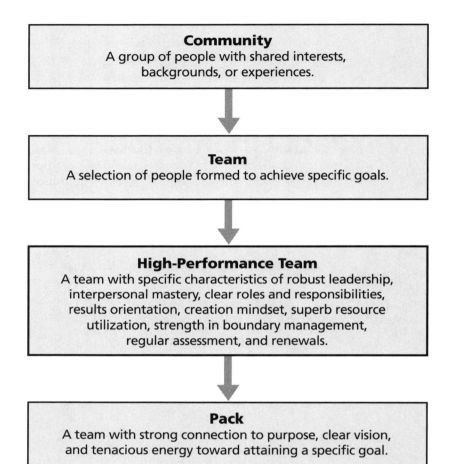

FIGURE 4.1   Differences between community, team, and pack.

PACK AS COMMUNITY

What makes wild dogs unique is that the pack is both a team and a community. A community is a collection of individuals with like interests and possibly shared backgrounds and histories. Communities are similar to clans and families, yet different in that family and clan membership is determined at birth. Pack membership is a conscious choice. An affinity group is a type of community wherein common interests are expressed and serve as the reason for coming together. Support groups and homeowner associations are types of communities.

In the least potent form, communities may be assemblies of like-minded individuals coming together in order to share experiences. We often see communities of people with similar desires uniting to maximize their effectiveness. Individuals in this case choose the community based upon fit and individual attractiveness to the community. Village and neighborhood communities, for example, form to bolster the common good. They build common areas such as parks and plant flowers in community gardens, all paid for by communal fees. If someone feels that the community does not have a direct and substantial personal benefit, that individual can withdraw support, either by moving away or by refusing to volunteer for non-compulsory activities.

We submit that a pack is a unique type of high-performance team and that the creation of a pack orientation and the leading of a pack are exceptional transformative leadership opportunities. In Chapter Five we address the creation process of a wild dog pack and discuss what differentiates the pack from other teams.

In addition to belonging to the high-performance team category, a wild dog pack could be described as a self-managed team.[1] We know from the literature that self-managed teams work best when they are composed of self-managed individuals (Mainz and Sims, 1989). Self-managed individuals take responsibility for monitoring their own performance, taking the proper corrective action, and seeking help, guidance, and the resources needed to get the task done.

A team is a type of community. Commonly leveraged in the work environment, teams bring forth stated goals with a focus toward achieving measurable gains. Many different types of teams exist—self-managing teams, quality circles, improvement teams, emergency response teams, crisis teams, functional product/service teams, cross-functional teams, task forces, investigative teams, crews, swat teams, and a host of others. A notable category is that of the high-performance team. The defining characteristics of high-performance teams include:

> *Robust Leadership:* Team leadership is competent and functioning. Leadership varies depending upon the skills needed for the situation. Each team member has the opportunity to exercise leadership when the situation warrants.
>
> *Quality Decision Making:* Decisions are always principle based and made by the appropriate individual, individuals, or team. Team decision making is of high quality, as evidenced by resulting performance. The team

builds its own ways of staying informed and gathering critical information. Securing information is a shared responsibility among team members.

Interpersonal Mastery: Relationships are open, honest, and direct. Strong, productive relationships are intentional. A high level of measurable trust is found within individuals, in dyads, and within the team itself. Risk taking and innovation toward building resilient relationships are rewarded.

Roles and Responsibilities Clarity: All members contribute and understand what is required from them and from each other. Individual mastery is apparent in both high- and low-skill tasks. Rewards are based upon the acquisition and productive utilization of skills beneficial to the team. Roles and responsibilities are well defined.

Results Orientation: Solid alignment exists to organizational purpose and vision. Goals are based upon achieving vision. A high sense of urgency to deliver results is visible, both for the short and long term.

Creation Mindset: The team is committed to a vision and aggressively approaches problems as opportunities to achieve that vision. Team members have the mental stance of owning the team results and its processes. No victimization is present. Problem-solving skills are high and effectively used.

Resource Utilization: All team members are valued and the team works to maximize the contributions of each member. An optimum balance is attained between team and individual development. Alignment of resources is based upon appreciation of the power of diversity, and unproductive traits or behaviors are readily called out.

Boundary Management: Interaction with other teams and organizations produces synergy toward objectives. Community is sought with customers, suppliers, up-line leadership, and other organizational participants.

Team Assessment and Renewal: Seeking improved results and attainment of team vision, team assessments and renewals occur on a regular basis. Quick response to improvement needs occurs.

DISTINCTIVE TRAITS OF PACKS

The ongoing study of why some teams are more effective than others, although helpful, is not new. Typically cohesiveness, group composition, leadership, motivation, group feedback, and communication have been found to positively impact team performance. For work teams, work-group autonomy, individual participation, knowledge diversity, and cohesiveness have been found to have a positive impact on team effectiveness.[2] While these are the traditional characteristics of team behavior, we argue that they are insufficient to understanding the current reality of a very successful type of team, the pack. The pack orientation and its leadership deserve a more in-depth study and application inquiry.

Independence and Coordination

Bookshelves are lined with a cornucopia of writings that address the issues regarding how to develop successful groups and teams. Critical to success is the selection of the most appropriate and advantageous type of team. Team purpose and the level of interaction among the members vary from team to team, as does the level of interdependence among the team members. These characteristics are significant in understanding the uniqueness of a team.

Writing nearly 30 years ago, Robert Kneidel described teams in terms of sport models. He contrasted the team profiles of basketball, football, and baseball.[3] Baseball teams are characterized by pooled interdependence (the individual efforts are aggregated) and by low levels of coordination. This explains why there are so many individual statistics in baseball, and why baseball pitchers command high salaries. Basketball and football teams have more interdependence and more coordination. Not knowing what type of team is needed is a major contributor to team failure. Attempting to win a world title football match using a baseball team mindset would be disastrous.

A pack is a highly interdependent and coordinated team, much like a basketball team, and the participants know this. The pack understands the importance of this relationship between coordination and interdependence. It forms the basis of their reality; they live it. In essence, wild dogs exist in community because of the coordination and interdependence that produces higher performance. Often individuals join a team or organization in spite of the coordination and interdependence components. How often have we found ourselves saying, "The work is easy, it's working with people that is the hard part."

A pack is a special and unique high-performance team (Figure 4.1). It is not simply the coming together of like-minded individuals or individuals with similar traits in order to align upon an acceptable vision. A pack is about the vision itself, and membership is reliant upon each member having the same clear vision. Like a pack of wild dogs after the prey, a pack within the organizational setting is intent upon its particular 'kill.' Subordinating "self" to the pack is easy, given that each member shares the pack's clarity of vision prior to joining.

Pack Purpose

Team distinctiveness is formed around the purpose of a team. In addition to a basketball team having a high level of coordination and interdependence, it must figure out its primary purpose. In college basketball, is the team's primary goal to win the NCAA championship, to have a high graduation rate, to not embarrass the school, to place players in the professional leagues, or to fill up the stadium?

Members of a pack place great importance upon clarity of purpose. In organizational terms, alignment to the pack's purpose is not a discovery process. It is the essence of each individual. As opposed to coming together to discover what we would like to create, the pack purpose is a manifestation of the individual's purpose.

Pack traits are more than just a set of shared traits. Packs go further. They not only share a set of traits, they form a community based upon these traits. Wild dog behavior for an individual joining a new organization or team would be to ask, "Where are we going? What is the goal?" Wild dogs would not ask, "How much is the pay?" More like the community of a family, members of the pack see membership as a primary reality, not a temporal choice.

Pack Leadership

One distinguishing trait of wild dogs is their ability to practice opportunistic leadership; depending upon what is needed at a given time, the animal with the appropriate skill for a particular situation becomes the leader.

Early research by Bowers and Seashore demonstrated that leadership behaviors could be shared in a work unit.[4] Some call it shared leadership, co-leadership, peer leadership, or distributed leadership. "At its heart is the notion that leadership is a collection of roles and behaviors that can be split apart, rotated, and used sequentially or concomitantly. This in turn means that at any one time multiple leaders can exist in a team, with each leader assuming a complementary leadership role."[5] It can occur when partners found a company, or through the merger of two companies. It works best when the leaders have different roles, or when, in the parlance of wild dogs, they hunt in different directions.

An example the authors describe in their article is Intel. "Gordon Moore was the long-term strategist and thinker, and Andy Grove was the short-term hands-on 'make your numbers guy.'"[6] This is radically different from the idea of *the* leader of an organization. Examples in the world abound. The success of Microsoft was due to Bill Gates *and* Paul Allen. Mike Ditka's 1983 Chicago Bears also had Buddy Ryan, the defensive coordinator. For every Moses, there is an Aaron. For Nelson Mandela, there was Steven Biko *and* Desmond Tutu. When the Miami Heat won the National Basketball Association championship in 2006, they did it with Shaquille O'Neal *and* Dwyane Wade.

Pack leadership works because of the commitment the individuals feel to the group. Wild dogs do not seem to care which one makes the kill; there are no special ceremonies for the dog that makes the first strike at the wildebeest. Wild dogs understand that the goal is to achieve success in the hunt, not to create a hero.

Packs also realize that the very concept of leadership might be strange. Who is actually in charge of the pack? Is it the alpha male, the head of the hunting party, or the animal that stays with the cubs? This is closer to the concept of autonomous leadership. Guzzo and Dickson use the label "autonomous work groups" to mean self-managing work teams. "These are teams or employees who typically perform highly related or interdependent jobs, who are identified and identifiable as a social unit in an organization, and who are given significant authority and responsibility for many aspects of their work."[7]

Pack Vision

Equally important as pack leadership is pack vision. Nutt and Backoff argue that the "key properties of a vision seem to be inspirational possibilities that are value centered and realizable, with superior imagery and articulation."[8] Collins and Porras, in their book *Built to Last*, describe a vision as an audacious goal and a vivid description. One of the biggest reasons why change efforts often fail is because there is no clear vision. "A vision says something that helps to clarify the direction in which an organization needs to move."[9] What many organizations think of as a vision statement is actually a strategic plan or an organizational goal. A vision must inspire. "A vision has a clear and compelling imagery that offers an innovative way to improve… a vision taps people's emotion and energy. When properly articulated a vision actually creates the enthusiasm that people have for sporting events."[10] While the research described was based on studies of organizations, the same could be said of teams. The concept of group potency is the belief that group members have the will to be successful. If group members think that they will be successful, then they will be.

Research has found that groups that set specific, difficult-to-reach goals were more effective than groups that had no goals. Collins and Porras, in their book *Built to Last*, call this having a 'Big Hairy Audacious Goal.' One example is Jack Welch's goal to make General Electric number 1 or number 2 in each product category or to sell or spin off the product. John F. Kennedy's goal for the United States was to put a man on the moon by the end of the 1960s and return him safely. Nelson Mandela's goal for South Africa was a smooth transition from apartheid to one-person, one-vote. Research has also found that groups that set their own goals produce results that are significantly better than groups that do not set their own goals.[11]

Drawing from the discussions above, a vision may be defined as a "big goal" captured in a vivid description. The pack vision for the wild dogs is the kill itself and preserving the pack for future survival. Individuals within the pack know that each kill is a win for the whole pack. In organizations, a "kill" may be an important sale or efficiency increase. Within the organization, some may not recognize that everyone benefits from success. They may believe that a promotion, compensation increase, or recognition is sourced by the hierarchy rather than from the business success itself. This kind of thinking leads to more of a lion culture, where some benefit significantly out of proportion to others, and where the rewards are not earned but bestowed. Sabotage of the team may occur when jealousy, envy, or resentfulness erupt.

For wild dogs, the vision is simple. It is the kill of an impala, a wildebeest, or a water buffalo, all of which are much bigger animals than a wild dog. The vision is a pack vision. All the wild dogs in the pack instinctively know that coordination and interdependence are needed to achieve the vision and that they, as evidenced by their group hunting characteristics, are committed to achieving the vision. If the wild dogs do not collectively believe they can kill their prey, the hunt will be futile.

Choosing a clear, simple vision by the pack can be difficult. Barry Schwartz, in his book *The Paradox of Choice: Why More Is Less*, points to the difficulty of having pack members pick a single vision. When a team is populated with members seeking to maximize every decision, intent on picking only the *best* solution, then the team suffers from inefficiency and/or deadlock. Instead, the course of discovering a vision that satisfies the expressed needs at hand leads to a focus without regret. Schwartz shares his perspective and insights on the hidden cost of having too many options:

> There is no denying that choice improves the quality of our lives. It enables us to control our destinies and to come close to getting exactly what we want out of any situation. Choice is essential to autonomy, which is absolutely fundamental to well-being. Healthy people want and need to direct their own lives.
>
> On the other hand, the fact that some choice is good doesn't necessarily mean that more choice is better. As I will demonstrate, there is a cost to having an overload of choice. As a culture, we are enamored with freedom, self-determination, and variety, and we are reluctant to give up any of our options. But clinging tenaciously to all the choices available to us contributes to bad decisions, anxiety, stress, and dissatisfaction—even to clinical depression.[12]

The individual freedom needed to promote conscious, empowered individuals sometimes can prevent the team from cementing a clear vision. The wild dogs choose a prey that meets their needs—available, vulnerable, and killable. Do wild dogs always pick the best prey? Probably not, but they don't become paralyzed in the choosing, frozen as the herd moves on. They choose a prey that meets their collective needs and proceed to the kill. Beware of over analyzing the choices in front of a team; move on to achieving success as your criteria outline.

WILD DOG CASE STUDY #2: THE DETROIT PISTONS

Imagine the setting: One team has two of the five best current players, four of the best fifty players ever to play the game, and a coach who has won eight championships. Another team is made up of castaways and no-names and a coach who had not achieved the same success of Phil Jackson. They come together to determine the best team in the league. Who wins? In 2004, the answer was the Detroit Pistons led by Chauncey Billups. They beat the Los Angeles Lakers in the National Basketball Association Championship. How did they do it? The Pistons were a pack of wild dogs.

The Pistons exemplified shared vision and shared leadership. There is a saying in sports, "feed the hot hand." Basically this means that everyone on the team should continue to pass the ball to whoever is playing well. It doesn't matter if it isn't the team superstar. If the goal is to win the game, players will do whatever it takes to win. That may mean that the superstar isn't the leading scorer. Well, ok. After examining the differences between the Lakers and the Pistons, we see that often it appeared that the superstars were more interested in scoring points than in winning the game.

The clearest evidence of the Piston's wild dog status is that Chauncey Billups was named most valued player for the series. He wasn't the team's leading scorer; that was Richard Hamilton. He wasn't voted on the all-star team; that was Ben Wallace. He wasn't even the biggest personality on the team; that was Rasheed Wallace. Yet Billups had the "hot hand" and his teammates gave him the ball. During their five games with the Lakers, either Shaquille O'Neal or Kobe Bryant was the team's leading scorer and only two other players ever scored more than ten points. For the Pistons, three different players were leading scorers (Rasheed Wallace, Richard Hamilton, and Chauncey Billups) and in every game at least three players scored more than ten points. In three of the five games, four players scored more than ten points.

In the aftermath, while the Pistons remained relatively intact as a team, the Lakers lost both Shaquille O'Neal (to the Miami Heat) and their coach Phil Jackson (to retirement, temporarily) during the off-season, making the Pistons the team to beat for the 2004-2005 season.

Action Opportunities

- Describe your present team using some of the concepts discussed.

- How robust is your team's vision? Is it your vision? How vivid is the description?

- How often is leadership, not just the title, shared, rotated, or distributed in your organization?

NOTES

1. (Mainz and Sims, 1989).
2. Cohen, S. G., & Bailey, D. E. (1997). What Makes Teams Work: Group Effectiveness Research from the Shop Floor to the Executive Suite. *Journal of Management, 23,* 239-290. Guzzo, R. A, & Dickson, M. W. (1996). Teams in organizations: Recent research on performance and effectiveness. *Annual Review of Psychology, 47,* 307-338.
3. Robert W. Keidel. Baseball, Football, and Basketball: Models for business. *Organizational Dynamics* (1984), Winter Edition, pages 5-18.
4. Bowers, D. G. & Seashore, S. E.; Predicting Organizational Effectiveness with a Four-Factor Theory of Leadership. *Administrative Science Quarterly,* (11, 238-263), 1966.
5. Barry, D.; Managing the Bossless Team - Lessons in Distributed Leadership, *Organizational Dynamics, volume 20,* 1991, pages 31-47
6. O'Toole, J., Galbraith, J. & Lawler, III, E. E. (2002). When Two (or More) Heads Are Better Than One: The Promise and Pitfalls of Shared Leadership. *California Management Review* 44: 65-83. (O'Toole, Galbraith, and Lawler, 2002: 75).
7. Guzzo, R. A, & Dickson, M. W. (1996). Teams in organizations: Recent Research on Performance and Effectiveness. *Annual Review of Psychology,* 47, 307-338.
8. Nutt, P. C. and Backoff, R. W. 1997. Crafting a Vision. *Journal of Management Inquiry* 6: 308-328.
9. (Kotter, 1995: 63).
10. (Nutt & Backoff, 1997: 309).
11. O'Leary-Kelly, A. M. Martocchio, J. J., and Frink, D. D. 1994. A review of the influence of group goals on group performance. *Academy of Management Journal* 37: 1285-1301.
12. Schwartz, B. (2004). *The Paradox of Choice: Why More Is Less.* HarperCollins, New York, page 3.

5

How to Create a
Pack of Wild Dogs

KNOWLEDGE POINTS

- Teaming stages include: Getting Together, Getting Down, Getting Real, and Getting Results.

- Your conscious will is your key asset. Wake up!

- Leadership is helping others to become conscious of their purpose in life.

- Sustainable alignment is the act of painting a compelling, collective vision that allows you and other conscious people to create.

- Conflict within a team is to be valued. Conflict holds meaning for the team and it is necessary for moving to Getting Results.

INTRODUCTION

So the question remains, "What is the process needed to create a pack of wild dogs?" The answer to this question depends upon your starting point. If you are starting as a zebra, you must first determine your purpose and vision. Lost in the herd, you may find the inquiry unimportant as you simply follow the masses...doing as the other zebras do. A key distinction between wild dogs and zebras is that wild dogs hunt a specific animal. They are after something. To become a wild dog, you must first ask yourself what you are hunting for. Why is this objective important to you?

If you are starting as a cheetah or a lion, the question becomes, "Why hunt with others?" Why not hunt alone? Or should you be an opportunist, forming temporary hunting alliances? While these questions seem quite obvious, many people rarely ask them. Let's first look at the teaming process and then see where these questions come in to play.

TEAMING LIKE WILD DOGS

High-performance teams have a natural progression from creation to the production of high-quality results. There are several good models available, but these often lack sufficient emphasis on leveraging conflict in order to move from chaos to high performance. The fundamental paradigm for many is that conflict is undesirable and should be avoided. However, in order to achieve the promise of high performance, a team must be willing to utilize the predictable conflict to gain a deeper understanding of each individual and thus open the team to discover the common base. The common base is the collective common will that serves as the engine for results production. The common will can be viewed as the collective spirit.

The steps to producing a high performance team—a pack of wild dogs—are as follows (also see Figure 5.1):

Getting Together: Forming the team means deciding upon the purpose of the team and its expected output. Why form the team? What can the team accomplish that couldn't be done by individual decision makers? The propensity to jump to team formation is sometimes without merit. In our current organizational climate, team decision making can be a biased vehicle. In addition to individual decision making, the option of ad hoc teaming often is overlooked in favor of established or standing teams. Find the team structure and membership that best fit the team's purpose. Many options exist and experimenting is permissible.

Getting Down: When conflicts appear, the tendency is to retreat to a pseudo community state where team members focus on getting along. The reminder that 'we're all on the same team' causes members to fall back to a polite state without a breakthrough to performance. Many people confuse consensus with the absence of conflict. In reality, great packs have high degrees of consensus and conflict. The conflict, however, is related to the task and not to the personalities.

At this juncture, the team faces a critical decision. Is performance important enough that members get real with each other? Or is the drive to work through and benefit from conflict subordinated to the wish to be genteel? There is a false choice between facing up to conflict

FIGURE 5.1 How to form a pack of wild dogs.

and valuing individuals. The team can display civility and respectfulness while at the same time unearthing and dealing with areas of disagreement.

Getting Real: Working through conflict means bringing to consciousness the authentic, individual will of each team member. Coming clean with individual motivations allows the discovery of the common will. Self-mastery is required. If individuals are confused and unconsciously conflicted, the mission to ascertain collective will may be unnecessarily complex. Knowing one's purpose in life and how one connects with the group is crucial. The role of high-performance individuals in producing a high-performance team becomes obvious. The success of a pack of wild dogs depends upon individuals understanding themselves to a high degree.

Getting Results: Working through conflict offers the promise of increased understanding about what the team has willpower to create. This greatly reduces the unconscious agendas that are so destructive to teaming. Once the common base or common will is ascertained, an alignment of individual purposes gives birth to results. The formation of a true community is at hand. It may mean revisiting the original purpose of the team, using new lessons about individual and collective will. A re-chartering may be in order. The leader must make certain that the results meet the expressed chartered intent.

We utilize the compass rose symbol to represent purpose. It can represent a single team member's purpose or that of the entire team or organization. Pointing to true north, it denotes the reason for being. The *Getting Real* illustration shows an individual bringing into consciousness his life's purpose.

CONSCIOUS, INDIVIDUAL WILL

The *Getting Down* stage of teaming is where significant decisions are made. It's necessary to avoid retreat to the initial congenial state of *Getting Together* and avoid moving too quickly to *Getting Real,* where the tough work of addressing conflict is present. A conscious, collective will is needed to produce high-performance results, and this is made possible in the *Getting Real* stage. But the collective will is inevitably attached to the individual will. Also, the importance of individual will is apparent in the role of the individual wild dog team member trait of tenacity. Without a robust will, the determination to achieve extraordinary performance fades. What is this thing called will?

More than a desire or wish, the concept of will speaks to action. Will is our creative spirit at work. Will is far from a declaration, it is the results themselves…our will is the manifestation of our true spirit. Our will is evident in the lives we have formed and the results we have created to date. Our will is found in all of our results…the good, the bad, and the ugly. We, as individuals, base our choices upon will. Sometimes the will is unconscious…which can be terribly confusing.

As an individual, I might proclaim my desire to lose some body weight. After several weeks of dieting, I may, in fact, have gained. Although serious about the desire to loose weight, I may have unconscious internal wills driving my eating habits. Maybe I quiet anger with food, or soothe disappointment. It's fruitless to remove myself from responsibility for the weight gain and attribute the gain to others or to my metabolism. I control what goes into my mouth and the amount of energy I expend through exercise. Yet upset by the weight gain, I look for a reason. In truth, the reasons are within, all thrown together in my subconscious. It is critical to first bring these hidden wills to the surface and resolve the internal conflicts. Weight loss will occur not through self-control, but by way of developing self mastery in the understanding of my will. This will lead to a more conscious exertion of willpower.

Beyond weight loss, where does my anger come from? From without? From where does my intolerance emanate? From the surrounding circumstances? No, anger, intolerance, and other emotions come from within. This does not mean that enormous barriers to my will do not exist. They do. Circumstances may call upon me to exercise colossal self will or to opt for an alternative internal will. In the final analysis, it is my will that responds, conscious or unconscious. It is not the barriers or even the opposing wills of others. These conditions may require an evaluation of how much energy I choose to expend, but the response is mine. It is interesting to note that we tend to attribute success to the workings of our wills. When we fail, it's easy to point to someone or something else that produced the poor results.

To unravel the complexity of conscious and unconscious will, we suggest that you must first determine your purpose in life. This is not a small task, but by choosing to bring a conscious life purpose to the surface, you create a broader context.

To help you answer this question are the thoughts of Viktor E. Frankl, who wrote *Man's Search for Meaning.* Frankl, an Austrian psychiatrist during World War II, survived three years in Auschwitz and other Nazi concentration camps. He developed a remarkable perspective on the psychology of survival and wrote about his imprisonment and other horrific experiences after studying individuals in the camps.

What Frankl learned was that when individuals discovered a reason to live, they were better able to endure and find a way to survive. We will say that again…individuals who had a reason to live found a way to live. After the war, Frankl established the meaning-centered psychotherapy called logotherapy, the therapy of meaning. Logotherapy focuses on our very reason for existence, not on secondary rationalizations of instinctual drives and desires. In the wild dog analogy, one way to guarantee you that you make the kill is to determine the meaning for your own life. From his text:

> As each situation in life represents a challenge to man and presents a problem for him to solve, the question of the meaning of life may actually be reversed. Ultimately, man

should not ask what the meaning of his life is, but rather he must recognize that it is he who is asked. In a word, each man is questioned by life; and he can answer to life by answering for his own life; to life he can only respond by being responsible.[1]

Frankl says that it is up to each of us to determine what we want to hunt for in our own lives. In a sense, we are all looking up at the heavens wondering, "Why am I here?" On our death beds the question would be, "What did my life mean; what was my reason for living?" The universe replies, "Good question!" What do you think the meaning of your life is? Once you figure it out, you must be responsible to your calling. It is your answer for your life, not anyone else's life. Whatever you want, hunt it with will.

Frankl gives additional insight to discovering our purpose in life:

According to logotherapy, we can discover this meaning in life in three different ways: (1) by creating a work or doing a deed; (2) by experiencing something or encountering someone; and (3) by the attitude we take toward unavoidable suffering.[2]

The first way is through achievement, the second is a deep understanding of love. The third way is where we seem to have difficulty. It deals with discovery through the pain of life. Suffering provides an opportunity to find the meaning for self. Recall our "jail theory of leadership." Frankl's message is consistent with the leadership approaches of King, Gandhi, and Mandela.

Why Are You Here?

A simple way to bring your will to bear is to ask yourself, "Why am I here?" When you walk through any door, ask the question. When you walk into a team meeting ask, "Why am I here?" Understanding the relationship between your presence in a meeting and your life's purpose brings forth a powerful, conscious spirit. Without the connection you're a zebra, going to the meeting because you were told to go. When you walk in the door of your home, ask the question, "Why am I here?" If your unconscious speaks, your answer may be, "Because this is where I live." But if you're connected to a conscious life purpose, the answer may be that you have a family to nurture or that you're choosing rest in order to fulfill your life's purpose. Operating out of a strong consciousness of your life's purpose, you will be surprised at the many options for achievement available to you. Act out of an unconscious zebra (or even a zombie) state of mind, and you may be surprised at how the world presents you with problems. Consciousness to life's purpose is a choice.

CONSCIOUS, COLLECTIVE WILL

Like the individual, the team has a collective will, conscious or unconscious. In part, the uniqueness of a wild dog team derives from the strength of its collective will. With even partial understanding of your individual will, you bring a level of self-mastery to the team that can be built upon. A wild dog team finds significant overlapping of these individual purposes. The alignment toward a specific goal is not so much out of the emergence of an attractive goal as it is from the belief that the goal is aligned with your life purpose. It is the gathering of sentient beings with a common will that produces a magnificent hunt. Your choice of hunting companions comes with the understanding that a conscious, collective will is a requirement of grand accomplishment. In a sense, you walk into the meeting room knowing why you are there and why the other team members are there. This convergence of purposes can yield astounding results.

If you are a cheetah, you may already have a purpose in life but be missing companions for the hunt. Why hunt with others? For you, the concept of alignment of wills to detect a common will is applicable. If a leader must tell his followers what is important in life, there may be a fall back to supporting zebra behavior. In a pack of wild dogs, the leader relies on the willfulness of the followers, seeking the consciousness of each individual to the goal.

These two different approaches were first outlined in the text *Work Miracles*.[3] In the traditional model of alignment (Figure 5.2), individuals come to an endeavor misaligned. Individual arrows point in every direction. Through the influence of a leader, the arrows become parallel. The leader puts the followers into alignment. The operational mindset is that the leader will bring you to the Promised Land; you need only conform and follow. Unfortunately, the previous structure eventually returns, with arrows pointing in every direction. The state of alignment depends upon the presence of the leader, on his or her charisma and ability to keep others in check. Alignment breaks down in the absence of the leader.

The vision is compelling when the leader paints the picture, but the internalization is shallow because it is generated outside of the individual. The group may feel an idolization of the leader, an unhealthy dependence. If a generous leader plays the part of a good

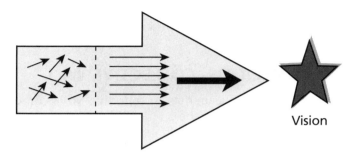

Vision

FIGURE 5.2 Traditional model of leader role with followers.

parent, the results may be acceptable to the followers. On the other hand, the group may have a lion-leader who demands the lion's share of rewards, recognition, and growth. A flip of the coin reveals the underlying purpose of the leader, and the team members are just zebras following the herd.

Another leadership approach holds a different mindset (Figure 5.3). People enter organizations with differing levels of consciousness. Some understand why they are there, having made the connection to a life purpose. Individuals with a high level of self mastery and are shown with the solid line. Where the individual consciousness is weak, the leader aids in the self-discovery process, increasing consciousness. The leader might simply ask the big question of each individual in the beginning, "Why are you here?" The leader would then seek their understanding of how the presented team vision might fit into the fulfillment of their life purpose.

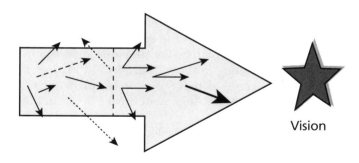

Vision

FIGURE 5.3 New model of leader or alpha dog role.

For some the connection may be strong, for others weak. In some few cases the vision may be significantly out of alignment with their purpose. It is rare to find a 180° misalignment. More common is a lack of spirit toward the vision when measured against where the team member is heading in life.

The leader wants to ascertain the level of alignment, the vector of energy each member has for the vision. The leader determines if the conscious collective will is adequate to accomplish the vision. It may be necessary to investigate another empowering vision available to the team. Adjustments to the vision may still meet the organizational purpose and inspire increased energy by team members. This is the generative process of a collective vision previously addressed. In short, the leader facilitates the team in discovering where they want to go and employs shared energy within the context of the larger organizational purpose. If certain members do not contribute significant energy toward a common vision based on common purpose, then suboptimal results may be expected. A wild dog leader will point the team toward success after first determining that individuals have an internal drive aligned with the vision and that the collective will is sufficient to accomplish the goals at hand.

Conscious wild dog team members don't follow simply because someone is the designated leader. They follow a leader who is skilled in bringing forth the collective, conscious will and the powerful alignment present in self. The alpha leader, the creator of the pack and establisher of social order, empowers individual team members by helping them better define their consciousness and passion.

For a cheetah-leader, we suggest this question for the emerging pack, "Why are you here?" Individual team members can answer only for themselves. Once your pack members have an answer, seek alignment. How can the conscious wills of all the members be made synergistic? Ask these questions again and again. "Why am I here? Why are you here? How are we aligned?" It's what you must do to develop your pack.

Some problems might arise. First, you might discover that pack members do not want to go where you want to go. This is where you reconsider your purpose. If your pack wants to hunt Kudu but you want to hunt Impala, the difference may not be significant enough to require the selection of different pack members. Where the difference in vision is significant, it may be necessary to find other members who share the common vision.

What if you are a lion-leader? Lion prides are characterized by laziness and lack of trust. A key question for the lion pride centers on how to build trust. Once again, the discovery of purpose is required. Trust is composed of three elements: consistency, commitment and capability. As outlined in *The Trust Imperative*,[4] the area of commitment is where purpose clearly emerges. Commitment is two-pronged. It includes commitment to the joint vision *and* commitment to each individual. In the case of the lion-leader, team members often question the commitment of the leader to them as individuals. This is where the lion-leader can leverage a transformation to pack leader. What is your commitment to each individual? If the level of commitment is shallow, distrust will prevail. However, if you view each team member as a beloved spirit, trust may blossom. Building trust is a big challenge for the lion-leaders.

SEIZING THE BENEFITS OF CONFLICT

To achieve a stage of high performance, *Getting Results* requires first the discovery of the team's will. It's necessary to transcend the difficult period of *Getting Down* and avoid retreating to characteristics of the forming phase, the *Getting Together* stage. As we have seen, the *Getting Real* stage is the way forward, seeking the alignment of individual, conscious wills to form a collective, conscious team will. When tensions arise in the *Getting Down* stage, the opportunity to grow presents itself. Tension often has its source in the unconscious will. By uncovering the deeper layers of the sources of tension and by seizing upon existing conflict, it's possible to experience a breakthrough in accessing the common will. This digging for collective will takes courage. Capitalizing upon conflict is a skill many teams fail to master, possibly due to their views of conflict itself.

Conflict is an inherent human condition. Too often the tendency is to avoid conflict within a team. The avoidance can emanate from a belief that a high-performance team needs the appearance of agreement, convergence, and harmony. When conflict naturally arises, there exists the inclination to be polite and take the conflict underground.

Teams can find themselves retreating to what Rodney King said, "People, I just want to say, can we all just get along? Can we stop making it horrible? We're all stuck here for a while. Let's try to work it out."[5] We are all stuck on the team, so can't we just get along? If the objective of the team is to appear in total agreement and of one accord, then the answer is 'yes.' But if the team is to be high performance, conflict is to be seized as an opportunity for discovery, for creation.

This is not to say that all conflict is healthy. M. Scott Peck points to an important distinction:

> Conflict may also be divided into that which is normal, necessary, healthy, and civil, as opposed to that which is abnormal, unnecessary, unhealthy and uncivil. It is vitally important to bear in mind that certain types of overt conflict are highly healthy, and civil, while either covert conflict or the absence of conflict may be most unhealthy and uncivil.[6]

Navigating conflict to produce productive outcome is a skill. Along the way to developing this skill, most will probably make a few errors. Although the concept of leveraging conflict in order to create a stronger team is not without risk, failure to address conflict will submarine a team.

WILD DOG CASE STUDY #3: THE IMPRESSIONISTS' HUNT; TRANSFORMATION IN THE ARTS

Paris has long been a center of both traditional art and innovation. It was in Paris, between 1874 and 1886, that eight unique exhibitions were held at irregular intervals. Several artists joined together, despite the harsh judgment of the conventional art society, to display something new. So unique were the pieces that the art establishment refused to support the exhibitions. Pierre-Auguste Renoir, Claude Monet, Camille Pissarro, Paul Cézanne, Edgar Degas, and Gustave Caillebotte were a pack of wild dogs collectively pursuing their passion for impressionist art.

When the first exhibit opened in a photographer's studio on April 15, 1884, it was without state aid or the approval of the French Institute. The powerful art establishment had neither sanctioned the event nor approved of the art. They understood and expertly commented upon Realism, Classic Modernism, and the evolution of Romanticism. This new type of art, both painting and sculpture, was…unfinished, simply an impression of what could be when properly refined and completed. The derogatory term 'impressionists' was employed by the art elite to describe this dreadful art form. To their dismay, this unflattering description was taken in hand by the new artists and lofted to a celebrated level.

In the study of transformation, the radical shift to the new is often initially held in contempt. Thus was the case with the impressionists in the later part of the nineteenth century. The impressionists displayed important attributes of a transformative leadership approach, that of a pack of wild dogs. As we have discovered, wild dog teams have as their characteristics individual contribution, pack vision, tenacity, and pack leadership. The impressionists displayed the unique characteristics of this type of high-performance team and transformed the art world.

When Monet, Renoir, Alfred Sisley, and Frédéric Bazille came together in 1862 in the studio of Gleyre in Paris, the brew of rebel impressionist was formulated.[7] In the summer of 1865, Monet, Renoir, and Bazille struck up a firm friendship, painting together in the open air in the village of Chailly-en-Bière.[8] Working in a space that was safe for expression without harsh criticism, the artists further explored their art.

Monet and Renoir, in particular, advanced their common interests in a new art form. Their bond came in large part from a common fervor, a mutual enthusiasm requiring expression. Honing their respective skills, each became a valued contributor to the emerging pack. On a high-performance wild dog team there are no low-performance individuals. It is true that a collection of high-performance individuals will not by itself produce a high-performance team, but the foundation of team excellence is found in individual excellence. Each impressionist stood as a master in his own right.

Years later when the expanding circle of artists displaying their works came together, it was not as a traditional organized group. They did not represent a formal society, complete with charter and drawn-out procedures. Instead, they shared a common commitment, painting outside the lines…or as the art critics might have said of their work, out of focus. The focus was not on hierarchical structure or on crafting dry formulation documents or on fighting over insignificant terminology. Their ardor for this impressionist art was their shared passion, their pack vision.

The impressionists clearly demonstrated the pack vision characteristic of a wild dog team. The basis for the deep-seated belief was born inside each artist. The desire to see the world through a new art style was found in each individually, not generated from any type of indoctrination. The artists discovered this common passion and then came together with the mission to expose their new style to the public at large.

The Parisian art establishment had other ideas. They believed impressionist art was an offense. Their opinions mattered in terms of financing, both in direct aid and in the approval stamp that facilitated display and enhanced purchase possibilities. The impressionists did not yield. Failing to bend under the weight of considerable criticism, the artists moved forward, exhibiting another wild dog pack characteristic, tenacity. When support did not materialize from the art establishment, the artists went ahead on their own. The first of the eight exhibitions, with no jury and no awards, must have caused quite a stir. So what! The public was attracted and the impressionists prevailed.

What about the leadership of this movement? Pack leadership was in full view, with situational leadership flowing from the common, internalized vision. An alpha dog provides the necessary stability and establishes the pack's order of operation, its acceptable behaviors and values. One can see Monet playing the role of alpha dog, setting the stage. But once the team was on the hunt, in this case producing a transformative shift in the art world, leadership emerged from all corners based upon need. The formation of the exhibitions streamed from many within the impressionist team. The conflict with the art establishment had many leaders. As opposed to the single-strong-leader blueprint used across many organizations today (lion leadership), the configuration of a wild dog team allows leadership to come from many quarters, offered with consistency of values and vision. It is found without the jealousy and ladder-climbing attributes of the lion-leader.

Today, impressionist art is a fully recognized and studied art form, but this was not always true. If not for a pack of wild dog artists intent on creating with an unprecedented art style, we would not be enriched with such beauty today. But what of the endless possibilities for other breakthroughs in all of life's concerns? Do you have some wild dog in you?

Action Opportunities

- What are the primary teams you currently participate with? In what stage of teaming does each of these reside? Write down how you could move these teams forward in their effectiveness.

- Where are you in conflict? If these areas and situations are just growth opportunities, what are the lessons being delivered to you?

- Where might accenting conflict be beneficial in your world? How can you leverage conflict in a particular situation?

- Take the Wild Dog survey (Appendix B). What is your area of opportunity?

NOTES

1.   Viktor E. Frankl, *Man's Search for Meaning* (Boston: Beacon Press, 1992, page 113).
2.   Viktor E. Frankl, ibid, page 115.
3.   S.K. Hacker and M.C. Wilson, *Work Miracles* (Blacksburg, Virginia: Insight Press, 1999).
4.   S.K. Hacker and M. Willard, *The Trust Imperative* (Milwaukee: Quality Press, 2001).
5.   The Rodney King Beating (LAPD Officers') Trial: In Their Own Words, http://www.law.umkc.edu/faculty/projects/ftrials/lapd/kingownwords.html
6.   M. Scott Peck; *A World Waiting to be Born: Civility Rediscovered* (New York: Bantam Books, 1993, page 216).
7.   WebMuseum, Paris; Monet, Claude http://www.ibiblio.org/wm/paint/auth/monet/
8.   Annie Perez, *Musée d'Orsay* (Paris: Jean-Christophe Castelain Publisher, 2005).

6

The Alpha Dog as Transformational Leader

KNOWLEDGE POINTS

- The alpha leader is responsible for setting social order and for bringing focus to conscious members of the pack.

- The Transformational Leadership Model speaks to the necessity for self mastery, people mastery and enterprise mastery.

- Management and leadership are different; great organizations need both.

- Transformational leadership is expressed through four sets of skill polarities: Energetic and Empowering, Analytical and Visionary, Administrative and Creative, Performer and Community Builder.

INTRODUCTION

In the creation of a wild dog team, a transformation from the existing organizational structure and performance must occur. Many different types of social structures exist, from affinity groups to ad hoc teams. A pack of wild dogs with the fever to pursue an inspiring vision needs an alpha dog, an alpha leader. This special kind of leader is needed to alter existing models and to move the group to a wild dog pack mentality. An alpha leader has the desire to build a team of conscious individuals with a pack vision and the internal drive to hunt down objectives with determination. In the previous chapter we outlined the process for generating such a team, from the *Getting Together* stage through the *Getting Results* stage. Now we will focus on the leader of such a change, the alpha dog.

REQUIREMENTS OF THE ALPHA LEADER

Strong situational leadership exists within wild dog hunts. The pack will chase a gazelle or an impala, taking its cues from various dogs as the hunt unfolds. Hunt leadership is determined by the position of the prey relative to the pack. All dogs are called upon at one time or another to demonstrate leadership. That is a key characteristic of the wild dog pack. Leaders step up from within the pack as needed. Within this same multi-leader pack, the creation of social order is the responsibility of the alpha male and the alpha female. The nurturing of the pups, the feeding sequence, and the mating order are all part of the pack's social structure. The alpha dog is the leader of this structure.

The alpha leader within an organization must create the pack, transforming the current team or group structure into something rather different. The alpha leader is obliged to be a transformational leader, employing distinctive skills and characteristics. He or she is to build a team with the attributes of pack leadership, pack vision, individual contribution, and tenacity. Despite the culture and systems in place that support old behavior, a new organization, the pack, will be brought into existence.

The alpha leader is there to transform the very nature of the team. Jim Collins, in *Good to Great*, refers to a Level 5 leader as the most successful business leader he found in his research. Of this type of leader, Collins says:

> We were surprised, shocked really, to discover the type of leadership required for turning a good company into a great one. Compared to the high profile leaders with big personalities who make headlines and become celebrities, the good-to-great leaders seem to have come from Mars. Self-effacing, quiet, reserved, even shy—these leaders are a paradoxical blend of personal humility and professional will. They are more like Lincoln and Socrates than Patton and Caesar.[1]

Collins captures the seemingly contradictory characteristics of the most successful leader when he says, "Level 5 leaders are a study in duality: modest and willful, humble and fearless."[2] Similarly, the alpha leader displays a complex array of characteristics and is capable of knowing what skills to bring to bear in various situations. These required skills are often thought to be diametrically opposed, at opposite ends of the spectrum. Key among these dualities is personal humility and tremendous willfulness. The lion-leader may exhibit willfulness but come up short on the humility side of the equation. Only through self awareness and authenticity does the transformational leader feel undisturbed in holding such disparate qualities.

Comprehending how such a leader is wired can be difficult. To help understand the nature of transformational leadership, we offer a model found in *Transformational Leadership: Creating Organizations of Meaning.*[3] The Transformational Leadership Model (Figure 6.1) is useful in its outline of the many different skills and characteristics of such a leader in the context of a living organization. The alpha leader must bring these skills and characteristics to bear in order to create a team of wild dogs, an organizational pack.

To create a pack of leaders, the alpha leader must radically alter the process of teaming. Recall that it is not the traditional leadership style of command and control that seeks to put people in alignment (Figure 5.2). Found in so many organizations are the products of lion-leaders and cheetah-leaders...teams with the focus on the leader, awaiting the leaders' instructions and inspiration. The result of this outdated approach is a diminished individual spirit that waits to be instructed by the leader.

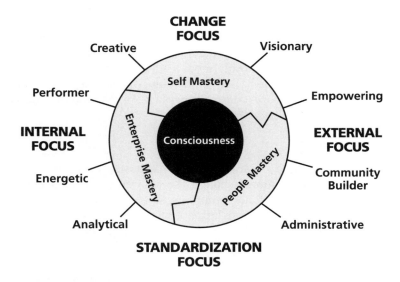

FIGURE 6.1 Transformational Leadership Model.

The alpha leader must change the team orientation to that of a pack. To transform the team is no small task.

Transformation has been defined as the marked change in the nature or function of organizational systems creating discontinuous, step-function improvement in sought-after result areas.

Transformational leadership is defined as leadership that goes beyond ordinary expectations by transmitting a sense of mission, stimulating learning experiences, and inspiring new ways of thinking.[4] The Transformational Leadership Model (Figure 6.1) seeks to synthesize the body of knowledge of radical improvement using a single integrated model. The model captures the need for transformational leaders to create personal and collective consciousness, to possess both an internal and an external focus, to understand that a continuum of change exists, to grasp the perspectives from which to view change, and to realize the polarity of skills required to lead transformational change.

TRANSFORMATIONAL LEADERSHIP

Designed to be holistic in nature, the Transformational Leadership Model draws upon the concept of a competing values framework in which the quadrants at first seem to carry a conflicting/opposing meaning.[5] The challenge is to see the particular skills required in each quadrant while standing in appreciation of the whole. Significant growth occurs through better understanding of how a leader integrates these skills.

We will now walk through the building of the Transformational Leadership Model and its components. Furthermore, we will examine the unique skills of a transformational leader. But before the skills can be effectively developed, let alone leveraged, the concept of consciousness of purpose comes into play. As previously outlined, individual consciousness is imperative.

Consciousness

Individual, group, and organizational consciousness (Figure 6.2) is at the heart of transformational change. An awareness of one's environment and one's own existence, emotions, sensations, and thoughts is a prerequisite to becoming a transformational leader. This is certainly the case with the development of a competent alpha leader. Clarity of purpose, values, and direction in life are imperative to deliberate and productive growth. Effective alpha leaders within organizations have developed self mastery and are clear about the connection of their personal vision with the vision of the organization.

FIGURE 6.2 Consciousness.

Consciousness of self opens the door to awareness or consciousness within the pack. As individuals join together with a pack vision, consciousness allows them to collectively monitor and openly discuss group behavior, attitudes, aspirations, opinions, motives, and judgments that contribute to or hinder the team's progress. The alpha leader sets the team's social order, making this level of self inspection customary. The conversations change as transference of blame and unhealthy dependence turn into understanding of the reasons why individuals create both success and failure.

Conscious individuals forming conscious groups working with shared vision toward a shared purpose are vital ingredients for creating a conscious enterprise. Consciousness of enterprise is seen when the entire organization has the ability to reflect and learn.

Rings of Mastery: Three Perspectives

Alpha leaders grasp three primary perspectives to be considered and influenced on the road to change. These perspectives are self mastery, people mastery and enterprise mastery (Figure 6.3). Self mastery includes clarity of purpose and vision. Walking through every door in life with a purpose is the hallmark of this level of consciousness. Engagements into the different venues of life are purposely sought. The alpha leader constantly checks results against pronounced intention to see whether they match and then asks, "If not, why not?" This is not living in a state of self judgment, but rather in quest of increased understanding of the connection between will, action, and result. In search of feedback, the leader desires other eyes to aid in sorting out will, action, and result. The leader regularly asks for feedback, advice, and alternative viewpoints to enhance self understanding.

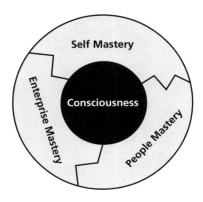

FIGURE 6.3   Rings of mastery.

For transformational leaders, self mastery extends beyond self to a commitment to walk with others on a path of self awareness. People Mastery is another consciousness perspective employed by the transformational leader. Collective consciousness surrounding relationships and the team is viewed as vital. The alpha leader promotes purposeful and healthy relationships with others, relationships in which all parties share an awareness of the connection created. Transformational leaders are engaged in the lives of team members, encouraging personal growth, feedback, and continuous learning through mentoring.

People mastery requires exceptional interpersonal skills: knowing how to build trust quickly and effectively, how to manage agreements, how to use a variety of communication styles, how to empathize where personal experience does not exist, and how to interact with others in their struggle for consciousness. Also called upon is the ability to develop an understanding of the attitudes, behaviors, beliefs, and assumptions of the collective and to have the collective see itself.

Enterprise Mastery entails collective consciousness of the people working within the organization and among its broader stakeholders. The organization as a whole knows why it exists, has a conscious sense of purpose, and utilizes a robust vision. Understanding the business is a key component of enterprise or business mastery. Here the word business is not limited to for-profit organizations. It refers to the value-added reason for the existence of the organization and the processes employed to generate the value add. The transformational leader views his or her role as that of a chief architect and engineer for extending the capacity of the business in order to deliver additional value to its stakeholder community. Enterprise mastery is evident in the skillful employment of strategic planning, holistic design, superior project execution, benchmarking, organizational culture construction, process improvement methodologies, evaluation, and performance measurement.

A challenge is found in the holding of multiple consciousnesses: self, relationship/team, and enterprise. Mastery in each of these areas is not so much a place of arrival as it is a distinction born out of demonstrated performance where the opportunity for improvement is infinite. The transformational leader, indeed an alpha leader, has mastery in each of these areas.

Internal and External Focus

Transformational leaders possess an internal and an external focus on the affects of transformative change (Figure 6.4). The internal view points to understanding and appreciating how to leverage change within the organization and the manner in which change is experienced by the people and systems within. The external view requires transformational leaders to understand how to impact persons and systems outside the organization and foretell the consequential reactions.

INTERNAL FOCUS ⟷ **EXTERNAL FOCUS**

FIGURE 6.4   Internal and external focus.

Focus on a Continuum of Change

The vertical axis of the model speaks to the continuum of change. The bottom of the axis speaks to standardization, the most subtle form of change. The top of the axis illustrates breakthrough change, or radical change focus. The full spectrum of change severity is found along the continuum.

**CHANGE
FOCUS**

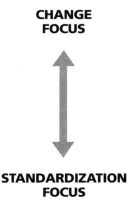

**STANDARDIZATION
FOCUS**

FIGURE 6.5   Continuum of change.

Transformational leaders are able to hold this continuum and polarity in mind and make decisions about the kinds of change needed to achieve the vision and goals of the organization. Transformational leaders recognize that standardization allows the organization to build upon a strong foundation of successful procedures while removing non-value-added variations in the performance of daily work. By contrast, continuous improvement efforts are aimed at achieving gradual, positive changes in performance, employing new methods and procedures. Finally, breakthrough efforts are intended to accomplish radical, step-function performance changes. Standardization falls within the realm of management and requires both an investment of the mind and a desire to remove system variations. Continuous and breakthrough improvement alike require transformational leadership…an investment of conscious commitment/spirit by an individual, group, and organization.

Skill Polarities

The leadership aspects noted in the model speak to the concept of polarity, two opposing attributes, tendencies, or principles. It is insufficient to achieve just one end of the spectrum. Rather, transformational leaders must discover and utilize the entire range. At times, the alpha leader displays skills at both ends of the spectrum simultaneously.

Here a distinction is made in the difference between a manager and a leader. Management may be defined as the effective and efficient use of resources to fulfill the organization's established vision and direction. Having a successful management function is critical to an organization's continued existence. Without management, transformational change will not take root. A well-managed foundation of systems and subsystems is crucial to ensuring the delivery of value-added products and/or services, but management is not leadership in total.

Peter Senge defines a transformational leader:

> Transformational leaders are designers, stewards and teachers. They are responsible for building organizations where people continually expand their capabilities to understand complexity, to clarify vision and to improve mental models.[6]

Yes, management and leadership are different. As Rick Griffin points out:

> Major management tasks can be viewed as planning, budgeting, organizing, staffing, controlling and problem solving. Likewise, key leadership tasks might be described as establishing direction, aligning people, motivating and inspiring.[7]

Both managerial and leadership skills are needed for survival. Leadership and management work together. Furthermore, Griffin states:

> Organizations need both management and leadership if they are to be effective. Leadership is necessary to create change, and management is necessary to achieve orderly results. Management in conjunction with leadership can produce orderly change, and leadership in conjunction with management can keep the organization properly aligned with its environment.[8]

What makes this peculiarity of managerial and leadership skills and characteristics even more interesting is that the transformational leader has working knowledge, if not mastery, of all the managerial skills as well as the leadership skills. In other words, the alpha leader can manage and also has leadership capabilities. There are four sets of polarities found in the transformation leadership model. Viewing these skills in a model form may be helpful (Figure 6.6).

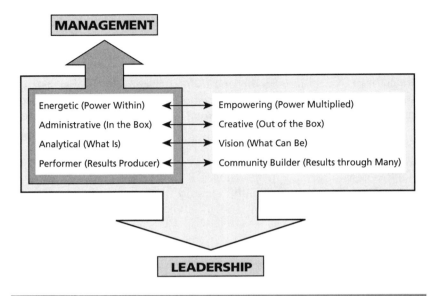

FIGURE 6.6   Skill set for management and leadership.

Let's further investigate the four polarities.

Energetic ←→ Empowering

Like the cheetah, many great managers have the ability to find and employ energy from within and to use this energy to knock down barriers in order to get the job done. This spring of individual energy seems to have great depth. Robust in nature, this energy source appears connected to an understanding of a larger purpose for self and a connection to a greater world. Clarity of personal purpose, vision, and values are critical to accessing, sustaining, and renewing energy from within. Personal mastery is in play.

Some people do not see themselves connected to the world. In particular, they do not see the role they themselves play in creating the pain, frustrations, and problems they have in life. These individuals seem to live at the mercy of life's events. They live in hope that good fortune will eventually arrive. The importance of will is minimized and they take a victim stance when things go badly.

In contrast, energetic people choose to see themselves linked to all that surrounds them instead of seeing no connection between their lives and the larger world. Their primary mental model is one of willful creation. They see themselves accountable for making things happen around them, the good, the bad, and the ugly. These individuals own it all, their failures and their achievements. Holding a causal view of themselves in the world, they draw energy from knowing that they always make a difference. Rather than experiencing depletion of energy as a result of failure and problems, these individuals use each opportunity to learn and to grow stronger. This is possible because their view of the world is that they themselves help create disappointment or failure. In the words of Joseph Pearce, "Our world to view is determined by our world view."[9] The depth of the spring of energy within is determined by our capacity to live and engage in life in a creative and causal manner.

Like the African wild dog, the transformational leader empowers others by creating alignment and attunement with a shared vision. The empowering leader promotes creativity, trust, unity, and opportunity to his or her staff as they work to achieve that shared vision. In our view, empowerment occurs only when others within the organization are connected to their own unique sense of purpose. Helping individuals to discover their life's purpose and how this is connected to their work is a new concept for many, as outlined by the alignment models (Figure 5.3). Leading others to consciousness is a key ingredient of empowerment. Leaders are required to understand the unique dreams and talents of their followers in order to achieve mastery in empowerment.

Administrative ◄──► Creative

Great managers have mastered the skill of administration, specifically an overall understanding of how the organization functions. This includes work systems, processes, people systems, and strategies for administrative control. The day-to-day job requirements of keeping the organization operational are well understood by the manager. Typically, control standards and performance requirements are established for the organization, the systems and performance allowing managers to correctly direct resources to the tasks at hand. Great managers use these standards as administrative controls to ensure that the organization achieves its overall strategy and vision.

In the daily world of administering the business, managers are called upon to 'work the system,' to get the desired results using defined processes. These managers may possess strong administrative skills but lack mastery in creativity. Like the African wild dog, the creative leader is inventive and innovative in finding solutions to problems.

Creativity most often happens when we do things about which we are enthusiastic.[10] This reinforces our view that transformational leaders must possess clarity of life purpose and the ability to coach others in the discovery of their life purpose. With this clarity in place at the individual and collective levels, the path to creativity is made wide for others to travel.

When engaged in creativity, it is important to remain conscious of the big sweeps of creation as well as the details. By being present to the power of creation and not driven by the past or the future, the creative juices are allowed to flow.

Creativity at the collective level may be limited or expanded by an organization's own view or preconceptions about *who* will be creative, *what* they will do, and *when* and *how* they will do it.[11] Transformational leaders are able to give up their preconceptions about who, what, when and how. Rather, they openly and graciously hold a world view that all human beings possess a unique creative essence that can and should be resourced. Encouraging risk taking and valuing lessons from all of life's happenings (including failure), the alpha leader builds collective creativity.

Analytical ◄──► Visionary

The analytical manager sees patterns and cause/effect relationships. He or she understands current results and reasons for existing performance. Managers use a number of related skills to analyze and better understand cause/effect relationships so that course corrections can be made. These related skills include, but are not limited to, research, budgeting, strategy, quality assessment, competitive analysis, benchmarking, and performance measurement. Performance measurement systems can be particularly powerful in bringing focus to several meaningful indicators that allow managers to understand how well the organization is performing.

While great managers often possess analytical and related skills in spades, these same managers may not have the visionary skills needed to lead transformation. In the course of researching the most successful companies of our time, we found vision to be essential to the success of an organization. According to Collins and Porras, the vision, the envisioned future, consists of two parts: an audacious goal and a vivid description.[12] At the level of the individual, a fundamental shift in one's relationship to results is needed in order to allow for the creation of audacious goals.

For many of us, our relationship to results was formed when we were school age children. We either made the grade or we did not, and we often endured the consequences of failure. Through the eyes of a child, not producing results often translates to "I must be stupid" or "Uh oh, I'm in trouble," irrespective of how parents or teachers react to the failure. It's important to not underestimate the influence this has on us as adults setting work goals. Many of us have spent years managing risk by imposing artificial limits on what we think we can achieve in order to assure that we always hit the mark.

Powerful visioning requires the willingness to dream, risk, and aspire to something greater that we think is possible. This can only be accomplished through a fundamental shift in our personal relationship to results. We must embrace failure rather than avoid it, seeing failure as an opportunity to learn and grow.

Like the cheetah, our primary relationship to producing results is personal, not collective. With great speed we attack the problem at hand and produce results; however, these results are often limited to the capacities of a sole individual. This, too, may be attributed to our years spent in the education system where, with the exception of team sports and music, we were measured on individual performance. By shifting our relationship to results from one of personal achievement to one of collective achievement, the alpha leader helps the pack envision a hunt of the largest of prey...setting audacious goals and achieving breakthrough results.

Vivid description is equally important in the visioning process. Many leaders truncate the visioning process or limit vision creation to the top management level, failing to involve the entire organization. This is why the vision may lack meaning and understanding for the rest of the organization. Visioning is more than printing up some slogans that have meaning for but a few. Visioning is painting a picture appealing to the array of our senses and emotions. The visioning process is also about listening. Have members of the pack describe the vision in their own words, attributing individual meaning to the attainment of the goals. Internalization is possible only when the pack can see the vision...a vision that includes them as an integral part.

Performer ◄──► Community Builder

The cheetah consistently achieves a high level of results as a single predator. The cheetah is a performer, doing the job of survival. High-performing managers are often distinguished by a proactive "can-do" attitude. Generally, they are highly organized around priorities. They seek to improve themselves through self study, personal and interpersonal mastery programs, and executive coaching. They believe that increasing personal skills and knowledge is the best way to achieve more.

Although personal performance sets a foundation for excellence, the skill of community building provides a multiplier effect. It can include relationships with direct reports, but it often extends beyond staff to include a broader group of people and organizations. Community building promotes trust and alignment, capitalizing on diversity to achieve greater goals. The essence of community building is the sense of oneness, seeing the connection of all, and having the skill to bring this realization of oneness to the community members. The alpha leader is a community builder, working to make connections to individuals no matter where they reside. Pulling in spirit and energy from multiple sources, this type of leader demonstrates the ability to find an unlimited supply of resources by simply connecting common interests.

Community builders may lead by example, making evident by their own performance the importance of the vision. Not stopping at being just an individual contributor, the community builder attracts others by asking what they wish to create and what they are willing to invest. Looking for these connections, rather than the contrasts in direction, is the work of the alpha leader. Peers are surprised by the wealth of contribution the alpha leader is able to garner in the pursuit of a large game.

LIFETIME CHALLENGE

Now we have the ingredients of the Transformational Leadership Model; consciousness in the center, three perspectives, internal and external focuses, continuum of change, and the four sets of polarity skills (Figure 6.7). It is a complete blueprint for an alpha leader, a lifetime challenge to be mastered by the transformational leader.

Organizations are filled with individuals with diverse skill sets. In some cases, individuals demonstrate strong managerial skills but lack the required transformational leadership skills. Promoting someone who possesses strong managerial skills without also assessing that person's leadership skills is a prescription for failure.

Understanding the differences between managerial skills and leadership skills opens the door to improved performance with regard to personnel management. The concept of combining technical development paths with leadership development paths has been introduced into many organizations. Many organizations make the effort to identify potential leaders, but the most promising aspect of performance enhancement has fallen short…building upon the diversity of the organization. When an organization can identify the skills and strengths of its members and develop the required alignment and supportive approach, it will see an explosion in the delivery of results.

Qualities of Transformational Leaders

Energetic: Possessing and exerting drive and enthusiasm. Discovering the power within, the internal force for achievement.

Empowering: Investing in others and fostering their energy toward a common vision. Aiding others in employing their power.

Administrative: Management of business affairs, working through the existing systems.

Creative: Ability to give birth to new ideas. Displaying originality, expressiveness, and imagination.

Analytical: Ability to understand what is, to grasp the elements that hold the present. Grasping why things are the way they are.

Visionary: Painting the future for others to see. Developing the attractive alternative of a better place.

Performer: Dependable achievement of tasks; accomplishment of one. Delivering upon individual commitments with excellence.

Community Builder: Results through many. Bringing the weight of common purpose into action. Employing the strength of individuals within and outside of the team/organization.

FIGURE 6.7   Transformational leader's summary of skills.

Transformation is a step-function change in desired performance results. To produce organizational transformation, strong transformational leadership skills are required. Unfortunately, many confuse managerial skills with leadership skills. They are different.

As we have seen, the Transformational Leadership Model describes the dynamic nature of transformation leadership and required skills. The model points to the additional skills a strong manager needs in order to demonstrate transformational leadership. Connecting this to the leadership development cycle, we see that one way to improve leadership skills is to identify weaknesses (which skills are missing) and develop those. Often we overplay our strengths, thinking that what worked in the past will work in the future.

As we coach children's basketball, we see that dribbling is the skill that separates great players from average players at a very early age

(8-10). Typically, a right-handed child develops an ability to dribble with her right hand. She may become the best dribbler on the team, skillfully dribbling to the basket and scoring most of the points. Instead of going on to develop other skills, such as learning to dribble with her left hand, that child may think that the key to success is to become a better right-hand dribbler. Eventually, by 10-13 years of age, that child's deficiency in other skill areas causes an overall decline in her ability to score points. The advice you might give that child is to develop left-hand dribbling skills. Although she may never be as good with her other hand, a little left-hand ability will make her overall skills even stronger.

The same is true of any individual. Even a little visionary skill will make someone's analytical skill more powerful. In short, find and develop your left-hand dribble.

Action Opportunities

- Assess your transformational leadership skill set. Where is your strength? Your opportunity?

- List the members of your enterprise's extended system and the value exchange between these entities and your enterprise.

- Who can you learn from in the areas of opportunity identified for yourself?

NOTES

1.   Jim Collins; *Good to Great* (New York: Harper Collins, 2001, page 13).
2.   Ibid, page 22.
3.   Stephen Hacker and Tammy Roberts, *Transformational Leadership: Creating Organizations of Meaning* (Milwaukee: Quality Press, 2004).
4.   James MacGregor Burns, *Leadership* (New York: Harper & Row, 1978).
5.   Robert E. Quinn, et. al. *Becoming a Master Manager: A Competency Framework,* (New York: John Wiley & Sons, Inc., 1996).
6.   Peter Senge, *The Fifth Discipline: The Art and Practice of the Learning Organization.* (New York: Double Day, 1990).
7.   Rick W. Griffin, *Fundamentals of Management: Core Concepts and Applications.* (Boston: Houghton Mifflin Company, 2000, page 301).
8.   Ibid, page 304.
9.   Joseph C. Pearce, *The Crack in the Cosmic Egg* (Three Rivers Press; Reissue edition, 1988, page 6).
10. Michael Ray and Michelle Myers. *Creativity in Business.* (New York: Broadway Books, a Division of Random House, 1986).
11. Alan Robinson and Sam Stern, *Corporate Creativity: How Innovation and Improvement Actually Happen.* (San Francisco: Berrett-Koehler Publishers, California, 1997).
12. James Collins and Jerry Porras, *Building Your Company's Vision.* (Harvard Business Review. Sept. – Oct., 1996).

7

Conclusion, Including a Defense of Zebras, Cheetahs, and Lions

KNOWLEDGE POINTS

- We do not think that wild dog pack leadership is *the* solution to organizational performance, we think it is *a* solution.

- Our support for that assertion comes from a variety of academic, practitioner, and business settings.

- Great leaders are like Noah – they take a lot of animals with them.

INTRODUCTION

By now you might think we are saying that the only way to be successful is to transform your team into a pack of wild dogs. As we conclude this book, we want to be clear: wild dog pack leadership is *an* answer to improving performance in an organization, it is not *the* answer.

First, if we were to make the statement that wild dog leadership was the answer, we would be out of alignment with our original aim of the book. Remember, we started this book by acknowledging the frustration leadership learners have; there are so many books claiming to be the definitive answer on leadership. We do not wish to add to this frustration. However, we do recognize that the world is evolving and that there will always be new problems that require new paradigms for performance.

We think that today's environment requires teams and other groups to form based on a shared vision, shared leadership, tenacity, and strong individual contribution. These are the traits of the wild dog. We also find numerous examples in history and a growing list of examples in modern times that exhibit these traits. In the book we feature five case studies. However, our research has identified dozens of additional organizations and groups that share these traits. These examples range from George Washington and the war of 1776 (see Appendix C) to Cirque Du Soleil to a recent start-up, the Lucina Company.

To develop the concepts of wild dog pack leadership, we tested our concepts numerous ways. The first question we asked: Can a pack of wild dogs really be compared to a human work group?

CAN WILD DOG TRAITS TRANSLATE TO HUMAN GROUPS?

A work group is made up of individuals who see themselves and who are seen by others as a social system, who are interdependent because of the tasks they perform as members of a group, who are embedded in one or more larger social systems (e.g. community, organization), and who perform tasks that affect others.[1] Even though a pack of African wild dogs cannot pass for Homo sapiens, it clearly meets the definition of a work group or a work team. Just as human work groups and teams operate within organizations, packs of African wild dogs are interdependent social entities that share responsibilities when they go on hunting expeditions.

Can the effectiveness of a pack of African wild dogs, with respect to hunting prey for food, be compared to the effectiveness of a human work team with respect to achieving organizational goals and objectives? Effectiveness may be defined as follows:

> "(a) group-produced outputs (quality or quantity, speed, customer satisfaction, and so on), (b) the consequences a group has for its members, or (c) the enhancement of a team's capability to perform effectively in the future."[2]

African wild dogs are the most successful predators in the animal kingdom. Their success stems from efficiency and effectiveness as they demonstrate group output. Each wild dog must live up to the expectations of the group or face the consequences of inadequate reward. Finally, the ability of the wild dogs to perform in future hunting expeditions improves as they participate in each hunting expedition.

The findings from the study reveal that the African wild dog characteristic of pack leadership could possibly be applicable to humans. If human work groups were as well coordinated as the African wild dogs, these groups could produce the same high-performance results.

In other words, the African wild dog traits could stimulate success within human work groups. African wild dogs instinctively organize themselves into social entities known as packs. Within the workplace (the jungle), they execute a task (catch a prey) and, ultimately, achieve a clearly defined goal (provide food for pack members). This process, instinctual in the African wild dog, is similar to what occurs with successful humans in the workplace (companies). They organize themselves into social entities (work groups) and work to execute tasks in view of achieving group or departmental objectives. Ultimately, the group actualizes well-defined organizational goals.

RESEARCH SUPPORT

We also wanted to test academically the concepts of pack leadership, pack vision, tenacity, and individual contribution. Specifically, we wanted to learn whether groups that have wild dog traits perform better than other groups. To test the concepts of wild dog traits on team effectiveness, we examined student work groups in a large southwestern university.

In this university, the students in the undergraduate business school enroll in a business policy class. A major component of this class is a business simulation game in which students are organized into groups of four or five to compete against other groups in decision-making. The teams whose companies make the best decisions are more profitable than the teams that do not make good decisions. We found this an ideal place to examine the wild dog characteristics and the link between these characteristics and group performance.

The sample population included 864 seniors who enrolled for the spring 2003 and the spring 2004 strategic management courses. These 864 seniors comprised 202 work groups of three to five members each.

Each work group or team in the sample population was faced with the task of establishing and running a business venture in the airline industry. The exercise is fully explained in the fourth edition of a book coauthored by Jerald R. Smith and Peggy A. Golden, *Airline: a Strategic Management Simulation*. The simulation was performed in eight rounds. During each round, the teams entered a set of decisions that they thought would make their airline successful, success being defined in terms of profitability. All the groups were after the same goal and only a limited number could attain it. The market could accommodate only a fixed number of airline seats; if one group sold more seats, the other groups sold fewer.

The teams performed one practice round in order to understand how the simulation program worked. Each team then completed a strategic plan prior to the first actual round of decision making. A survey was completed after the groups had made the first round of decisions, thereby ensuring that each group had ample time to work together as a collective. The dependent variable, the profitability of the group's airline, was evaluated after the fourth decision round. Because he had experience with the simulation, one of the authors could tell that some groups that were doing very badly had given up after the midpoint. Their performance worsened because they quit trying, not because they made bad decisions.

The survey in Appendix B was administered to these groups and the answers were correlated with how much profit a group had made after the fourth decision round. We found that teams scoring higher on pack and individual traits made more profit than teams that scored lower.

To determine the robustness of our results we ran additional analyses. One could argue that wild dog traits should be found in only the best teams and should predict differences between the best teams and all other teams, not just teams in general. To address this issue, we divided our sample into two groups, the top 20% in terms of profit and all others. The results are virtually identical to the previous results with one exception. When examining the best teams versus the worst teams, we see that pack traits are more of a predictor of high profit than individual traits.

In general, this research demonstrates that teams with a higher endowment of a specific set of pack and individual traits performed higher on a simulation exercise than other teams. When performance was separated into best teams versus all other teams, the pack traits were a better predictor of success than individual traits.

In addition to the research support for the concept, we started using the analogy in various consulting and teaching engagements. The analogy seemed to offer face validity in that individuals and companies felt that their organizations were acting like herds of zebra or that their ranks were filled with cheetah-leaders. As our clients demanded more understanding of the wild dogs, we started to develop the concept. This book is, in a way, a result of our interest in further developing the concept.

IN DEFENSE OF OTHER ANIMALS

We would be remiss if we didn't recognize that many of the best leaders are not "wild dogs." While this is not our point, we can identify leaders that might not be alpha dogs (Jack Welch, Bill Gates, Andy Grove, George Steinbrenner, Bear Bryant) and we can identify groups with lion-leaders or cheetahs-leaders that did great things (the Egyptians, the Ottomans, the Romans, and Chinese Dynasties).

We think there is a place for cheetah-leadership. Some organizations and teams need leaders who will inject a quick burst of energy to "jump start" the organization. Some organizations need lion leaders who are willing to "clean house" when necessary and develop enough power to overcome the internal problems in the organizations. All organizations can benefit from some level of zebra behavior. Zebras are communal and loyal and can operate with high levels of functionality. Even so, we argue that in today's environment, leveraging the formation of wild dog packs and alpha leadership holds the promise of transformative results.

We started this book by discussing the use and power of analogies. We then proceeded to develop an analogy of the African wild dog and we demonstrated how modeling behavior on this animal might help groups and leaders accomplish desired results. As we said earlier, we do not claim that this book is the last word on the subject of leadership. Being true to our word, we end with another animal analogy that that might also have insights into leadership.

Noah of Biblical times had his hands full with a diversity of animals. We believe that Noah was an alpha leader. Given the command to build an ark, collect a pair of each animal, and await a mighty flood, Noah faced a big challenge. What did he discover in his journey of transformational change?

Build the Boat

Noah's opportunity was with this assignment. The time, place, level of challenge, and impact on ego may have not been optimal in his view, but he moved forward. Of course, it didn't hurt that his boss did have a way with people…and a commanding voice.

The opportunity is now. Whatever role you play in whatever organization, take the initiative now…move to pack leadership environment. Often people say, "If only I could achieve the next level in the organization, then I would be able to effect change, to be the dynamic leader I desire to be." Take another look. Your current situation may be the best chance you have to demonstrate pack leadership. Failure to do so may spell the end of your upward movement.

Take All the Animals You Can

Noah had his hands full managing conflicts on board. Not everyone got along well…animals and people. The animals included natural enemies. And remember, Noah's three sons and their wives were on board as well. How would you like to spend months on a boat with your in-laws and a bunch of animals? But the common vision of staying alive seemed to galvanize the participants. All were needed to fulfill the mission.

Leaders need all the help they can muster, so be careful who you exclude from the group. Alignment is the critical element. Is there sufficient alignment in terms of the vision, values, and methods chosen to achieve specific goals? If so, then the remaining differences are potential assets…different viewpoints from which to accomplish the vision. And if not, then separation may be required. Indecisiveness and ambiguity surrounding who is on or off of the team can be a real barrier.

Be Bold; Noah Did Not Have a Degree in Ship Building

With neither a nautical engineering degree nor a lot of boat-building experience, Noah went for it. He started with some basic dimensions and learned along the way: "Make a boat from resinous wood, seal it with tar; and construct decks and stalls throughout the ship. Make it 450 feet long, 75 feet wide, and 45 feet high. Construct a skylight all the way around the ship, eighteen inches below the roof; and make three decks inside the boat – a bottom, middle and upper deck – and put a door in the side."[3] These specifications seem to leave a lot of critical details to be figured out. Sure, Noah made mistakes. It's likely he underwent some confidence plunges. The point is, he also had the wild dog characteristics of perseverance and tenacity. Even when it appeared the boat idea might just have been a bad dream, he kept on.

Pack leadership may be a new idea to you. Your present skills may be lacking. But improvement will not come through watching another inspirational video or engaging in intellectual discussions for amusement. Skill will come with practice, resulting in both successes and failures.

Getting instruction in golf is one thing. Skill development, however, occurs through hours on the driving range. Attending weight-loss seminars and reading diet books is good. Weight loss, however, occurs as a result of wise decisions made every day about food consumption and exercise.

Expect the Storm, That's Why the Ark

To flood the earth would take a little time, but rain was expected. Noah didn't expend his energy complaining about the rain; that would have been illogical. He made a plan, prepared for contingencies, and expected the hardships that were part of the price of achievement. He was prepared for rain and the ensuing flood. The ark was the vehicle to achieve an objective.

The investment in pack leadership is to create, to achieve something that is not currently a reality. Many challenges lay ahead…challenges in the form of opposing wills, barriers, resources, bureaucracy, politics, and competing priorities. Expecting the trials ahead, pack leadership looks to embrace the difficulties and leverage them where possible.

Expect the Rainbow and Dry Land; Success Is About Will

Noah learned the lessons of staying truthful to a calling. He did not sway from the task at hand, but rather pushed forward using his reserve of will. Building a huge ark on dry land, miles from any body of water, must have taken a great deal of will.

Our God-given gift of free will is often underutilized. Consciously employing our will toward great and challenging goals is a choice. Many choose to simply subordinate their wills to random environmental happenings. If beneficial and desired circumstances deliver themselves to the doorstep, then ok, they claim the credit. And if not, they find someone to blame for their misfortunes. An alternative to this thinking is to see the power of individual will and the power of the collective will. Noah did, and he ended up safe and dry, having been instrumental in saving life on earth.

The barriers may be underestimated and the energy needed to accomplish an objective more than anticipated, but success yields to will. Pack leaders focus on the object at hand and are clear with their precious willpower. "Want" may be what starts the hunt, but "will" is what delivers dinner.

Finally, we would be naive if we thought a pack of wild dogs was the answer to the question of how to be an effective leader. As the world changes, so too does our understanding of leadership change. It may be that wild dog thinking is a powerful tool for understanding how to become a better leader, but who knows? In years to come, we might be all thinking about how to be more like Noah.

Action Opportunities

- What worthwhile opportunities are in front of you and your team right now?

- What resources do you have? How can you expand those resources?

- What internal conversations hold you and your team back from being bold?

- What barriers do you face? What can be gained by overcoming these barriers?

- Read and do. Great resources exist for developing your skills to achieve top performance. Putting the readings to action is the hard part. Remember, until the rain actually came, all of Noah's work was just theory.

NOTES

1.   Guzzo and Dickson, 1996
2.   Guzzo and Dickson, 1996: 309
3.   *The Living Bible*, Tyndale House Publishers, 1971. Genesis, Chapter 6, verses 14-16.

Appendix A
Transformational Leadership Self-Assessment

In the following survey, you will be asked a series of questions to evaluate your skills as a transformational leader. Please read carefully and answer as honestly as you possibly can using the scale defined here.

1-2: that doesn't describe me at all
3-4: that describes me sometimes
5-6: that describes me a lot of the time
7: that describes me all of the time

Note that few people will have all 7s (or all 1s).

____ 1) Because of my skills, I am usually picked to be on major projects.

____ 2) I am not easily distracted.

____ 3) I am not nervous with having others responsible for my rewards.

____ 4) I enjoy achieving goals.

____ 5) I enjoy creating novel solutions to routine problems.

____ 6) I enjoy making goals.

____ 7) I enjoy solving problems.

____ 8) I enjoy solving complex problems.

____ 9) I enjoy the day-to-day tasks of keeping major projects on schedule.

____ 10) I enjoy working in an orderly fashion where goals and objectives are clear.

____ 11) I enjoy working long hours if I know it will lead to the desired output.

___ 12) I hate doing the same thing over and over.

___ 13) I need to understand how what I do fits into the big picture.

___ 14) I think there is a logical solution to all problems.

___ 15) I try to help others get their work done.

___ 16) In a project group, I would rather the group I work with be
   • happy and achieve satisfactory results than be unhappy and
   achieve outstanding results.

___ 17) People can depend on me to do what I say I will do.

___ 18) People would describe me as analytical.

___ 19) People would describe me as good at time management.

___ 20) People would describe me as capable and hardworking.

___ 21) People would describe me as creative.

___ 22) People would describe me as energetic.

___ 23) Understanding why I am doing a project helps me to do
   better.

___ 24) Who I work with is as important as the work I do.

___ 25) I'm able to communicate the importance of a major project to
   others who are working on it.

___ 26) With regard to a major project, I don't stop until it is done.

___ 27) With regard to a major project, I enjoy brainstorming new
   ways to implement and execute solutions.

___ 28) With regard to a major project, I keep a tight schedule of who
   is doing what.

___ 29) With regard to a major project, I look for people who have
   similar goals.

___ 30) With regard to a major project, I make sure everybody's
   contributing toward the overall goal.

___ 31) With regard to a major project, I make sure roles are clear.

___ 32) With regard to a major project, I make sure that people
   understand how the project is connected to their personal
   goals.

___ 33) With regard to a major project, I start project meetings
   reviewing the vision of the project.

___ 34) With regard to a major project, I think it is important for the
   people on the project to "bond" as a group.

___ 35) With regard to a major project, I think there is one best way
   (or solution).

___ 36) With regard to a major project, I try to find alignment between individual needs and the organizational needs.

___ 37) With regard to a major project, I work best when I have a close connection with the people I am working with.

___ 38) With regard to a major project, if I have finished my part, I help others do their part.

___ 39) With regard to a major project, people look to me to come up with unique ideas.

___ 40) With regard to a major project, people often ask my advice on how to proceed.

SCORING INSTRUCTIONS

For each characteristic, total your responses 1-7 for each relevant question (see below) and then divide the total by five (five is the total number of questions for each characteristic) to produce you average score for that characteristic. Determine what your strength area is (highest score) and your opportunity for growth (lowest score).

Performer:	Questions 1, 4, 8, 7, 20
Energetic:	Questions 2, 11, 22, 26, 38
Analytical:	Questions 7, 14, 18, 35, 40
Administrative:	Questions 9, 10, 19, 28, 31
Creative:	Questions 5, 12, 21, 27, 39
Visionary:	Questions 6, 13, 23, 25, 33
Empower:	Questions 3, 15, 30, 32, 36
Community Builder:	Questions 16, 24, 29, 34, 37

Appendix B
Wild Dog Self-Assessment

P lease read carefully and answer the following questions as honestly as you possibly can, using the scale of 1–7 as defined below.

1 = Disagree completely
2 = Disagree
3 = Disagree somewhat
4 = Neutral
5 = Agree somewhat
6 = Agree
7 = Agree completely

	1	2	3	4	5	6	7
1. I have the skills necessary to contribute to this team.							
2. I am committed to the success of my team.							
3. I believe my teammates want the team to be successful.							
4. I am confident in my abilities.							
5. The success of my team is very important to me.							
6. I believe my team will be very successful.							

	1	2	3	4	5	6	7
7. My team is made up of members with different skills and expertise.							
8. My team has a well-thought-out and clearly defined goal.							
9. Different team members volunteer leadership in their various areas of specialization.							
10. Communication and cooperation among my team members are excellent.							
11. I consider my team's goal measurable.							
12. I consider cooperation among my team members important.							
13. The leadership role is rotated in my team.							
14. If necessary, I will do more than my fair share of work to ensure the success of my team.							
15. Team members voluntarily pick up tasks they feel they can best execute given their skills, expertise, and abilities.							
16. I feel enthusiastic and motivated about my team's primary objective.							
17. I enjoy being a part of my team.							
18. I think our team will be successful.							

SCORING INSTRUCTIONS

For each characteristic, total your responses 1-7 for each relevant question (see below) and then divide the total by the number of questions for that characteristic to produce your average score for that characteristic. Determine what your strength area is (highest score) and your opportunity for growth (lowest score).

Pack vision:	Questions – 3, 6, 8, 10, 11, 16, 17, 18
Pack leadership:	Questions – 7, 9, 13, 15
Tenacity:	Questions – 2, 5, 12, 14
Individual Skills:	Questions – 1, 4

Appendix C
More Wild Dog Stories

GENERAL GEORGE WASHINGTON

If there ever was a pack of wild dogs born of hardship and a bellyful of defeat, it would have been the leadership of the American army under General George Washington in its beginning year. Declaring independence from the Crown in 1776 was but a paper exercise, one that was to be heavily contested with the ax of war.

King George III called upon Parliament to teach the rebellion a lesson that would serve the empire as a whole. Well funded and full of contempt for the ragtag traitors, the British military leadership came after the farmers, the tradesmen, and the other simple people of the breakaway colonies. Loyalists in the new world spied and provided support as the British landed and challenged the rebel force with a vengeance.

William Howe, the British commander, led redcoats and Hessian mercenaries that surpassed Washington's ragtag citizen army in both numbers and skill. Washington's army, a band of over-confident boys with no military experience at the signing of the Declaration of Independence, fought the most powerful nation on earth and finished the war a brotherhood of fighting patriots.

In Boston, the clever American leadership ousted the British in a strategic move. But the severe and deadly losses of New York, Fort Washington, Fort Lee, and New Jersey and the near collapse of the army itself due to sickness, poor equipment, disillusionment, and short enlistments presented arguably the darkest time in American history. Indeed, the British had already acknowledged victory in the campaign, needing only a mop-up effort with the last of the rebels.

What, then, created a sustained, emboldened threat to the superior British force in early 1777? To what may we attribute the threat that would result in eventual colonial victory and the signing of the Treaty of Paris in 1783? In a daring move, Washington and his officers led their army back across the Delaware River on Christmas night in the middle of a winter storm to attack Hessian troops in Trenton, New Jersey. This unexpected victory and a battle outside of Princeton with Cornwallis's troops solidified the resolve of Washington and his men to never surrender. This was the wild dog characteristic that won the day and won the war…tenacity. As David McCullough captured in his popular book, *1776*:

> "He was not a brilliant strategist or tactician, not a gifted orator, not an intellectual. At several crucial moments he had shown marked indecisiveness. He had made serious mistakes in judgment. But experience had been his great teacher from boyhood, and in this his greatest test, he learned steadily from experience. Above all, Washington never forgot what was at stake and he never gave up.
>
> Again and again, in letters to Congress and to his officers, and in his general orders, he had called for perseverance – for "perseverance and spirit, "for "patience and perseverance," for "unremitting courage and perseverance." Soon after the victories of Trenton ad Princeton, he had written: "A people unused to restraint must be led, they will not be drove." Without Washington's leadership and unrelenting perseverance, the revolution almost certainly would have failed. As Nathanel Greene foresaw as the war went on, "He will be the deliverer of his own country."[1]

During the first year of war against the British Empire, Washington had created the one weapon insurmountable to superior forces…a pack of wild dogs with everything to lose. His tenacious, supportive leadership style overcame a greater opposing force…and his leadership deficiencies.

LANCE ARMSTRONG AND USPS CYCLING TEAM

To further illustrate the concept of wild dog leadership, we can look to Lance Armstrong and his six Tour de France cycling victories. In the history of the sport, Armstrong is the only person to ever win six Tours. We suggest that one of the reasons he was so successful was his creation of a pack of wild dog companions.

Although cycling is really is a team sport, only one rider eventually wears the yellow jersey. The amazing story of Lance Armstrong has been chronicled on video and in his first book, *It's Not About the Bike.* Armstrong, a good rider, wasn't the best. Just about a year before his first Tour de France win, he was diagnosed with cancer. Throughout his disease, recovery, and therapy, Armstrong found the will to become arguably the greatest cyclist of all. His book touched us....the good guy strives to be all that he can be and his hard work pays off. However, in his second book Armstrong sets the record straight about his accomplishments.

While he recognizes that he is a strong contributor, Armstrong also makes the point that cycling is a team sport and that he is only great because he has a great pack. In his latest book, *Every Second Counts,* Armstrong talks about the tension between individual and team effort. He says, "It takes eight fellow USPS riders to get to the finish line in one piece, let alone first place. I only deserve the zipper. The rest of it belongs to the other guys." He talks in his book about the various skills on the team. Three of the riders on the teams that won the first two Tour de France championships were good enough, Lance felt, to be "lead dog" on their own teams. He remarked how it was a testament to their dedication to the team (shared vision and tenacity at work) that they rode so hard on his behalf. Other team members, whom Armstrong referred to as "domestiques," performed other essential roles such as riding interference and ferrying food and equipment to Lance when it was necessary.

Here we see evidence of individual commitment and shared vision, because the less skilled riders still had a job to do and they did it well. Armstrong also talks about the pain they experienced when one of his pack left to ride on another team. "It was as if Colin Powell might as well have signed on to help the Chinese." This shows strong shared vision. In the book, Armstrong talks about the shared leadership between his teammates, the team tactician, and himself as they plot their strategy to ensure that Armstrong would be victorious. He devotes several chapters to describing how he picks his wild dogs and how new packs are formed. He talks about how Tyler Hamilton, one of his main rivals in his quest for 6, was "stolen" from him by another team, and the contribution that a great team makes to its leader.

Armstrong also raises an interesting question regarding who is the alpha dog. He mentions several times throughout the book that the leader of the team is Johan Bruyneel, who played the role of tactician, or *director sportif.* Bruyneel, a former cyclist, once beat the great Miguel Indurain. More than one story in the book tells of Bruyneel, via radio communications, giving instructions to Lance and his team regarding strategy. One of these stories demonstrates what it means to be the alpha dog. During one of Armstrong's quests for the victory, his team was badly hurt. There were numerous injuries and they were down by more than 13 minutes to Jan Ulrich's team. At this point, over one of the grueling mountain stretches, Bruyneel suggested that the team "play dead." His idea was that if they looked as though they were hurt and tired, the Ulrich team would pedal hard to get away from them. The strategy was to make the Ulrich team expend energy and then have Armstrong's team "sneak up and snatch victory." Of course it worked!

Armstrong was the alpha dog. He determined the mindset of the team, decided upon staffing and roles. Bruyneel was the leader of the tactical plan in the midst of the hunt...the one who saw clearly the lay of the land while the alpha dog joined on the hunt. Armstrong took direction from Bruyneel, as Bruyneel served as the situational leader.

NOTE

1.   David McCullough, *1776*; (New York: Simon & Schuster, 2005, page 293).

Appendix D
Pack Leadership Lessons from the Wild Dogs of Africa

Although not particularly beautiful, the wild dogs of Africa are the most effective predators on land. With a kill ratio of approximately eight kills out of every ten hunts, they rely upon the pack structure to bring down large antelope. Through perseverance, they accomplish hunts lasting as long as three days. Large antelope, exhausted by such a long pursuit, eventually succumb to the pack. Individual skills and ongoing contribution are required from each member of this high-performance team. At the same time, nurturing the young is a pack endeavor, as the pack understands its future depends upon its future hunters.

Key characteristics are:

Pack Vision   Pack Leadership

Individual Skill   Tenacity

Key Learnings:

- Be clear about what you're hunting.
- Identify your potential pack of wild dogs.
- Empower individuals to join the hunt.
- Launch the attack.
- Stay with the prey until the job is completed.

ALIGNMENT AND ATTUNEMENT

Traditionally, individual arrows point in every direction. Through the influence of the leader, all arrows become parallel. The mindset is that the leader will bring you to the Promised Land; you need only conform and follow. However, soon after this parallel alignment, the previous structure returns, with arrows pointing in every direction. The conformity breaks down. The story is convincing enough to inspire conformity, but before long our lives move us away from that conformity. Leadership: manipulative, programming.

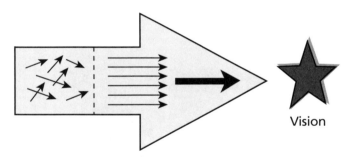

Vision

Traditionally, individual arrows point in every direction. Through the influence of the leader, all arrows become parallel. The mindset is that the leader will bring you to the Promised Land; you need only conform and follow. However, soon after this parallel alignment, the previous structure returns, with arrows pointing in every direction. The conformity breaks down. The story is convincing enough to inspire conformity, but before long our lives move us away from that conformity. Leadership: manipulative, programming.   People enter organizations with different levels of consciousness. The leader's role is to aid self discovery and increase consciousness. The leader accepts different burning platforms, capitalizes on vector energy, points towards goals, and inspires common energy (alignment) to drive

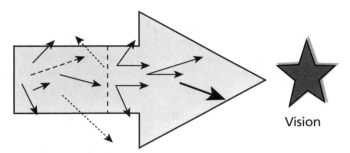

Vision

towards that common goal, all the while recognizing individuals. A leader helps people know what they want and use shared energy for the good of the organization. The attunement process then lets people buy into each other's direction and fine tune how they use their energy for their interests. Individuals determine what role the organization plays in his or her life, what he or she is energized by.

TEAMING

High-performance teams have a natural progression from creation to results. In order to achieve the promise of high performance, a team must be willing to utilize the predictable conflict to gain a deeper understanding of each individual, opening the team and making it possible to discover the common base, the collective common will that serves as the engine for results. The steps to high performance are as follows:

 **Getting Together:** Forming the team means deciding upon the purpose of the team and its expected output. Often the option of ad hoc teaming is overlooked in favor of established teams. Find the team structure and membership that best fit the team's purpose. Many options exist and experimenting is permissible.

 **Getting Down:** When conflicts appear the tendency is to retreat to a pseudo community state where team members work to get along. The reminder that 'we are all on the same team' causes a fall back to politeness without a breakthrough to performance. A critical decision faces the team. Is performance important enough to cause members to get real with each other?

 **Getting Real:** Working through conflict means that team members must expose their true objectives… bringing to consciousness the authentic will of each team member. Coming clean with individual motivations allows the discovery of the common will.

 Getting Results: Once the common base, the common will, is ascertained, an alignment of purposes leads to results. The leader must make certain the results being produced will meet the chartered intent.

TRANSFORMATIONAL LEADERSHIP MODEL

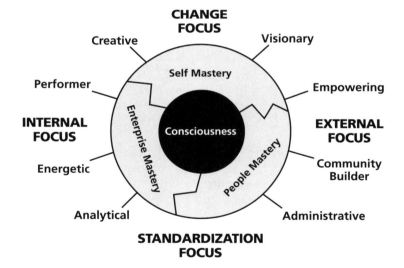

Leadership and Management are valuable skill sets and are different in nature. Both are needed within an organization.

Management is concerned with stewardship of systems and subsystems…bringing order to chaos and providing structure. A standardization focus is prevalent; reduction of variation is the target. Management is of the mind.

Leadership is concerned with change, creating the future for the organization. Leadership is of the spirit. A keen sense of self and high interpersonal skills are required to effectively lead.

Four sets of polarities exist in the model, each offering a pair of contrasting skills. The challenge for a successful manager is to take on a leadership position and embrace all four of the polarities.

DEFINITIONS

Creative – (Outside the box) The ability to be inventive, to think in a non-linear manner. Imaginative, innovative, and inspired thoughts are aspects of the creative mind.

Administrative – (In the box) Supports existing processes in the drive for predictable results. Manages the processes and applies productive control. Holds self and others accountable to agreed upon procedures. Understands current system status.

Visionary – (What can be) Sees a compelling future; proficient in articulation coupled with a reason for departing from the current state. Has a living experience in the vision, revealing connection with multiple senses.

Analytical – (What is) Sees patterns and cause/effect relationships. Understands current results and reasons for existing performance. Measures, collects data, converts data into information and provides insight into the information.

Performer – (Results producer) Displays internal drive derived from knowledge of want and/or purpose. A doer, not spectator. Consistently achieves high level of results on a personal basis. Individually a significant contributor in all undertakings.

Community Builder – (Results through many) Builder of trust and communal purpose. Capitalizes upon diversity while focusing upon contribution. Seeks and discovers persons and/or groups with similar values and interest. Forms alliances, partnerships, teams, and unions to achieve mutual goals.

Energetic – (Power within) Strong in finding the energy and power from within. Has strong capacity for knocking down barriers, for moving through adversity. Upbeat, and alive.

Empowering – (Power without) Produces alignment and attunement toward a shared vision. Displays enabling skills in an adult-adult relationship. Aiding in the discovery of power found within others for their life purpose.

Bibliography

Armstrong, Lance and Sally Jenkins. *Every Second Counts*. New York: Broadway Books, Division of Random House, 2003.

Barker, Joel A.; Discovering the Future: The Business of Paradigms, *Charthouse International Learning Corporation Video*, 1990.

Barry, D.; Managing the Bossless Team - Lessons in Distributed Leadership, *Organizational Dynamics, Volume 20*, 1991.

Bowers, D. G. & Seashore, S. E.; Predicting Organizational Effectiveness with a Four-Factor Theory of Leadership. *Administrative Science Quarterly*, (11, 238-263), 1966.

Burns, James MacGregor. *Leadership*. New York: Harper & Row, 1978.

Cohen, S. G., & Bailey, D. E. (1997). What Makes Teams Work: Group Effectiveness Research from the Shop Floor to the Executive Suite. *Journal of Management, 23.*

Collins, Jim. Interview; *Fast Company*, Issue 51, October 2001.

Collins, Jim; *Good to Great*, New York: Harper Collins, 2001.

Collins, James and Porras, Jerry; Building Your Company's Vision; *Harvard Business Review;* Sept. – Oct., 1996.

Frankl, Viktor E.; *Man's Search for Meaning*, Boston: Beacon Press, 1992.

Griffin, Rick W. *Fundamentals of Management: Core Concepts and Applications*. Boston: Houghton Mifflin Company, 2000.

Guzzo, R. A, & Dickson, M. W. (1996). "Teams in organizations: Recent research on performance and effectiveness." *Annual Review of Psychology, 47.*

Hacker, Stephen and Tammy Roberts. *Transformational Leadership: Creating Organizations of Meaning;* Milwaukee: ASQ Quality Press, 2005.

Hacker, S.K. and M.C. Wilson. *Work Miracles.* Blacksburg, Virginia: Insight Press, 1999.

Hacker, S.K. and M. Willard. *The Trust Imperative.* Milwaukee: ASQ Quality Press, 2001.

Keidel, Robert. Baseball, Football, and Basketball: Models for business. *Organizational Dynamics* (1984), Winter Edition.

Kotter, John. *Leading Change.* Boston: Harvard Business School Press, 1996.

Leadership and Organization Development 26 (5) 400-411; *Public Service Management Journal and Measuring Business Excellence;* 8 (3).

Living Bible, *Tyndale House Publishers,* 1971. Genesis, Chapter 6, verses 14-16.

McNutt, John and Leslie Boggs. *Running Wild: Dispelling the Myths of the African Wild Dogs.* Smithsonian Books, 1997.

Morrell, Margot and Capparell, Stephanie. *Shackleton's Way: Leadership Lessons from the Great Antarctic Explorer.* New York: Penguin Putnam, 2001.

Nutt, P. C. and Backoff, R. W. 1997. Crafting a Vision. *Journal of Management Inquiry 6.*

O'Leary-Kelly, A. M. Martocchio, J. J., and Frink, D. D. 1994. "A review of the influence of group goals on group performance." *Academy of Management Journal 37.*

O'Toole, J., Galbraith, J. & Lawler, III, E. E. (2002). When Two (or More) Heads Are Better Than One: The Promise and Pitfalls of Shared Leadership. *California Management Review* 44: 65-83. (O'Toole, Galbraith, and Lawler, 2002: 75).

Pearce, Joseph C.; *The Crack in the Cosmic Egg.* Three Rivers Press; Reissue edition, 1988.

Peck, M. Scott. *A World Waiting to be Born: Civility Rediscovered.* New York: Bantam Books, 1993.

Perez, Annie; *Musée d'Orsay;* Jean-Christophe Castelain Publisher; Paris 2005

Quinn, Robert E., et. al. *Becoming a Master Manager: A Competency Framework.* New York: John Wiley & Sons, Inc., 1996.

Ray, Michael and Michelle Myers. *Creativity in Business.* New York, 1986.

Robinson, Alan and Sam Stern. *Corporate Creativity: How Innovation and Improvement Actually Happen.* San Francisco: Berrett-Koehler Publishers, 1997.

Schwartz, B. *The Paradox of Choice: Why More Is Less.* New York: HarperCollins, 2004.

Senge, Peter. *The Fifth Discipline: The Art and Practice of the Learning Organization.* New York: Doubleday, 1990.

Washington, Marvin. and Hacker, Marla. 2005. Why change fails, understanding the importance of knowledge in implementing change. *Leadership and Organizational Development,* 26 (5) 400-411

Worsley, Frank A. *Shackleton's Boat Journey.* New York: W. W. Norton & Company, 1977.

Winters, Dick. *Beyond the Band of Brothers.* New York: Penguin Group, 2006.

WEBSITES

Conservation Spotlight: Wild Dogs. Excerpted from S. Rotz Mamakos, *AZA Communiqué, Dec 1996;* http://www.umich.edu/~esupdate/library/97.01-02/mamakos.html

PBS's Nature: *Cheetahs in a Hot Spot.* http://www.pbs.org/wnet/nature/cheetahs/hunters.html

IUCN, The World Conservation Union, Cat Specialist Group, 1996 http://lynx.uio.no/catfolk/afrleo02.htm

The Cyber Zoomobile. http://home.globalcrossing.net/~brendel/lion.html

(http://www.dtngroup.com/sdkids/kids/animals/lions)

Woolf, Norma Bennett; http://www.canismajor.com/dog/afriwild.html

The Rodney King Beating (LAPD Officers') Trial: In Their Own Words, http://www.law.umkc.edu/faculty/projects/ftrials/lapd/kingownwords.html

WebMuseum, Paris; Monet, Claude http://www.ibiblio.org/wm/paint/auth/monet/

Index